A PORTRAIT OF INTERCESSION

A Portrait of Intercession

Mark D. Spencer

Cover design by Jesse Spencer and The Design Aesthetic at WWW.THEDESIGNAESTHETIC.COM.
Author's photograph by Paige Fagre

The King James Bible is the translation used throughout this book unless noted. (The author has chosen to capitalize nouns and pronouns pertaining to the divine Name.)

Other Scripture quotations are taken from the following:

NLT – Scripture quotations marked by NLT are taken from the Holy Bible, New Living Translation, copyright ©1996. Used by permission of Tyndale House Publishers, Inc. Wheaton, Illinois 60189. All rights reserved.

NIV – Scriptures taken from the Holy Bible, New International Version®, NIV®. Copyright © 1973, 1978, 1984 by Biblica, Inc. Used by permission of Zondervan. All rights reserved worldwide.

NASB – Scripture quotations taken from the New American Standard Bible®, Copyright © 1960, 1962, 1963, 1968, 1971, 1972, 1973, 1975, 1977, 1995 by The Lockman Foundation Used by permission. (www.Lockman.org)

The Amplified Bible – Scripture taken from the Amplified Bible, Copyright © 1954, 1958, 1962, 1964, 1965, 1987 by The Lockman Foundation. Used by permission.

The Living Bible – Scripture quotations marked "TLB" or "The Living Bible" are taken from The Living Bible [computer file] / Kenneth N. Taylor. © electronic ed. Wheaton : Tyndale House, 1997, ©1971 by Tyndale House Publishers, Inc. Used by permission. All rights reserved.

THE MESSAGE – Scripture taken from The Message. Copyright © 1993, 1994, 1995, 1996, 2000, 2001, 2002. Used by permission of NavPress Publishing Group.

Order this book online at www.trafford.com
or email orders@trafford.com

Most Trafford titles are also available at major online book retailers.

Printed in Victoria, BC, Canada.

ISBN: 978-1-4269-2266-4 (sc)
ISBN: 978-1-4269-2267-1 (hc)

Library of Congress Control Number: 2009912309

Our mission is to efficiently provide the world's finest, most comprehensive book publishing service, enabling every author to experience success. To find out how to publish your book, your way, and have it available worldwide, visit us online at www.trafford.com

Trafford rev. 02/03/2010

 www.trafford.com

North America & international
toll-free: 1 888 232 4444 (USA & Canada)
phone: 250 383 6864 ♦ fax: 812 355 4082

ALSO BY MARK D. SPENCER

The Cry for Spiritual Reality
Surely God Will Do Me Good!

ACKNOWLEDGMENTS

"...and be ye thankful!"

My heartfelt thanks

...to Pat Lockridge for her years of encouragement, help and prayer concerning my writing.

...to David Williamson for his friendship and motivation to complete this project.

...to all the faithful prayer warriors and intercessors at Inner Court with whom I have had the opportunity to flesh out my Christian experience.

...to my son Jesse for his cover design.

...to my wonderful wife Patty, and my son Matthew for their tireless editing, advice and encouragement along the way.

Dedication

...for the Chief Intercessor, the Lord Jesus Christ, and His Helper, the Holy Spirit. May this book be used by Them to call forth a people of prayer!

"This One (the Holy Spirit), the only present Intercessor on earth, has no hearts upon which He can lay His burdens, and no bodies through which He can suffer and work, except the hearts and bodies of those who are His dwelling place. Through them He does His intercessory work on earth, and they become intercessors by reason of the Intercessor within them." Norman Grubb from the book, *Rees Howells Intercessor*.

Contents

Preface

One of the outstanding intercessors of the 20th Century was Rees Howells from the nation of Wales. During the darkest hours of the Battle of Britain Rees made this comment, "Suppose millions prayed but no one believed?" The company of intercessors that the Spirit of God had assembled around him pressed in to the deeper things of God, often at great personal expense. Their dedication and personal sacrifice enabled them to lay hold of God's manifold promises and they often directed the course of the war from their corporate prayer closet in Swansea.

While claiming no equality with such outstanding believers, none-the-less it is my hope that *A Portrait of Intercession* will on some level stir to the depths of their being those whom the Spirit of God has called to this life changing and world changing ministry of prayer.

A Portrait of Intercession is collection of articles, often prophetic in nature dealing with various aspects of intercession. Each chapter will at once challenge the believer to go not only the first mile with Jesus but willingly and joyfully press on in true and vital overcoming faith to go the second mile with Him in prayer and intercession.

A Portrait of Intercession is a series of challenges, calling the believer to stretch out in believing and bold faith to "be strong, to know their God, and do exploits" in Jesus' name.

A Portrait of Intercession is a call to a more intense and intimate relationship with Jesus; to see His vision for the nations and to hear His heart for the peoples of the world.

In this hour of history, the Spirit of God is looking for those who will dare to believe and know the extraordinary goodness of our God. It is then these believers yielded to and taught of the Spirit, who the Lord will Himself believe through so that the peoples of world might see and experience the extraordinary greatness of our God!

Intercession is, of necessity, often a hidden ministry. Its labors may be seen by few on earth but it is readily recognized and welcomed at the

Throne of Grace. It is possibly the most noble of ministries and surely the most noble of the various forms and sorts of prayer. You see, intercession willingly joins us with Jesus in His never ending, ever watchful prayer for and over His people. It is a selfless praying which readily enters into Christ's sufferings (that is, our joining with Him in His divine laboring at the expense of our own wants and desires). Together, let's prepare our hearts for the call of the Spirit into this "prince of ministries."

Let us never be turned back by the challenge or apparent difficulties facing us as we walk with Christ in His high priestly prayers. Our love for Jesus compels us to "pray without ceasing" and bear what only He can sustain us in and through, bringing us to the completion of His awesome purposes in the earth – "souls from every nation."

Shall we go, for He is waiting?

The Essence – The prayer of intercession is not for the fearful nor is it prayer for selfish gains or ends. It is a bold praying that dares enter into the sufferings of Christ. It is a prayer that abandon's itself to the Great Intercessor. But it is also praying rich in the intimacy of the Christ Himself who ever lives to make intercession for us! It is a prayer that willingly enters into the agonies of Christ's own prayer in order to identify with those for whom it seeks answers. As such, it is a guarded prayer in that at its end is the authority and manifestation of the risen Christ Himself!

one

A PORTRAIT OF INTERCESSION

INTERCESSORY PRAYER IS RADICAL prayer. It is not for the faint hearted or for the weak.

And from the days of John the Baptist until now the Kingdom of Heaven suffers violence and the violent take it by force.

MATTHEW 11:12

Finally, my brethren, be strong in the Lord and in the power of His might. Put on the whole armor of God, that you might be able to stand against the wiles of the devil.

EPHESIANS 6:10-11

Intercession touches the heart of God as it pulls down strongholds within men's hearts and within the heavenlies.

For the weapons of our warfare are not carnal, but mighty through God to the pulling down of strongholds, casting down imaginations, and every high thing that exalts itself against the knowledge of God, and bringing into captivity every thought to the obedience of Christ.

2 CORINTHIANS 10:4-5

Intercession prepares the way for God's Spirit to woo and lead men to Christ. It opens the doors of opportunity to proclaim the Gospel to those who were once deaf and blinded to the love of God found in Christ.

Continue in prayer, and watch with thanksgiving, praying also, for us, that God would open a door of utterance, to speak the mystery of Christ.

COLOSSIANS 4:2-3

Intercession opens the windows of heaven, not only for spiritual blessing, but for the releasing of financial and material blessing. It will establish the young one who is being tossed to and fro. It will settle the restless and disgruntled. It will not give up until the desired results are obtained.

And He said unto them, "Which of you shall have a friend, and shall go to him at midnight, and say to him, 'Friend, lend me three loaves of bread; for a friend of mine in his journey has come to me and I have nothing to set before him?' And he, from inside shall answer and say, 'Don't trouble me for the door is now shut and my children are with me in bed; I cannot rise and give what you desire.' I say unto you, though he will not rise and give him because he is his friend, yet because of his importunity he will rise and give him as much as he needs. And I say unto you, (keep on) asking, and it shall be given you, (keep on) seeking and you shall find; (keep on) knocking and it shall be opened unto you. For everyone that asks receives, and he that seeks finds, and to him that knocks it shall be opened."

Luke 11:5-10

The intercessor understands intensive labor and the struggle for life and death. Natural birth and development comes through labor and struggle. Spiritual birth and development is no different.

My little children, of whom I travail in birth again until Christ be formed in you.

Galatians 4:19

Intercessory prayer will develop your character and then prove your mettle.

That the trial of your faith, being much more precious than gold that perishes, though it be tried with fire, might be found unto praise and honor and glory at the appearing of Jesus Christ.

1 Peter 1:7

Intercessory prayer will stand in the face of adversity and not back down. Men will be offended at the intercessor's boldness and his utter confidence as he places demands upon the Covenant. It is better to offend men than to offend the heavenly Father!

And going away from there, Jesus withdrew to the district of Tyre and Sidon. And behold, a woman who was a Canaanite of that district came out and with a loud, troublesome cry begged, 'Have mercy on me, O Lord, Son of David! My daughter is miserably and distressingly and cruelly possessed by a demon.' But He did not answer a word. And His disciples came and implored Him, saying, 'Send her away; for she is crying after us.' But she came and kneeling, worshipped Him, and kept praying, 'Lord, help me!' And He answered, 'It is not right to take the children's bread and throw it to the little dogs.' She said, 'Yes, Lord, yet even the little pups eat the crumbs that fall from the young master's table.' Then Jesus answered her, 'O woman, great is your faith! Be it done for you as you wish.' And her daughter was cured from that moment.

Matthew 15:21 – 28 Amplified

The intercessor finds no shame or makes no apology in proclaiming the Gospel of Jesus Christ.

For I am not ashamed of the Gospel of Christ for it is the power of God unto Salvation to everyone that believes, to the Jew first and also to the Greek.

Romans 1:16

Whosoever, therefore, shall be ashamed of Me and of My words in this adulterous and sinful generation, of him also shall the Son of Man be ashamed, when He comes in the glory of His Father with the holy angels.

Mark 8:38

For we do not have a High Priest who is unable to be touched with the feeling of our infirmities, but was in all points tempted like we are, yet without sin. Let us, therefore, come boldly unto the throne of grace that we may obtain mercy and find grace to help in time of need.

Hebrews 4:15-16

Effective intercession cannot be done without the aid of the Holy Spirit! It will rely upon the Unseen Partner, the Advocate. It looks to the unlimited resources and bounty of an Almighty God.

Likewise, the Spirit also helps our infirmity for we know not what we should pray for as we ought, but the Spirit Himself makes intercession for us with groanings which cannot be uttered. And He that searches the hearts knows what is the mind of the Spirit, because He makes intercession for the saints according to the will of God.

ROMANS 8:26-21

Now to Him who, by and in consequence of the action of His power that is at work within us, is able to carry out His purpose and do superabundantly, far over and above all that we dare ask or think - infinitely beyond our highest prayers, desires, thoughts, hopes or dreams,

EPHESIANS 3:20 AMPLIFIED

Intercessory prayer will defy circumstance and obstacles far too powerful and overwhelming for ordinary men. Jesus said,

If you will believe, all things are possible to him that believes.

MARK 9:23

Intercessory prayer believes God! Intercession moves immovable mountains, conquers unconquerable situations! Intercessory prayer obtains God's perfect will!

And this is the confidence that we have in Him that if we ask any thing according to His will, he hears us; And if we know that He hears us, whatever we ask, we know that we have the petitions that we desired of Him.

1 JOHN 5:14-15

If you abide in Me and My words abide in you, you shall ask whatever you will and it will be done unto you.

JOHN 15:7

When others have long since given up because they have reached the end of themselves, the intercessor throws himself upon the mercy of God and draws unlimited strength, stamina and endurance from Him who is Strength.

I can do all things through Christ who strengthens me.

PHILIPPIANS 4:13

His grace becomes our sufficiency. Our weaknesses become His strength!

2 CORINTHIANS 12:9 Author's paraphrase

As the intercessor is hidden away with the Lord, in that secret place of the Most High, strengths are exchanged – mine for His and His for mine. The waiting upon God becomes a delightful thing, a joy only a privileged few will ever know.

They that wait upon the Lord shall renew (exchange) their strength. They shall mount up with wings of eagles, they shall run and not be weary, they shall walk and not faint.

ISAIAH 40:31

Intercessory prayer unites the believer with the Lord of the Harvest. Imagine being a co-laborer together with Him; a joint heirs with Christ!

Ask of Me and I will give you the nations for your inheritance and the uttermost parts of the earth for your possession.

PSALM 2:8

Take My yoke upon you, and learn of Me; for I am meek and lowly in heart, and you shall find rest for your souls. For My yoke is easy and My burden is light.

MATTHEW 11:29

The secret of the Christian life and the often perplexing ministry of intercession has been discovered – learning of Him! Not from others. Not from a book about Him, but from Him. The Lord's nature and mind becomes the believer's. Jesus' characteristics become his. Christ's thoughts become his. As he learns these secrets, he is able to then entrust the Lord with every challenge faced.

Casting all your care upon Him for He cares for you.

1 PETER 5:7

The intercessor becomes meek and lowly in heart. Not believing he can carry the burden alone, the intercessor casts His Spirit-received burden back upon the Lord. The yoke of the Lord Jesus becomes easy and His burden is then light. The Lord is now carrying the brunt of the weight. It is His labor and His work that have now been entered. The intercessor's life is now simply yielded to the Master, to flow and follow His lead, His direction and will! Christ's work is now accomplished His way and in His time. The intercessor now finds he is laboring within the rest of God and he is carried along by the anointing of the Spirit.

> *There remains, therefore, a rest to the people of God. For he that is entered into His rest, he also has ceased from his own works as God did from His. Let us labor, therefore, to enter into that rest...*
> HEBREWS 4:9-11A

The call has long since gone out. The eyes of the Lord are looking for those who will answer the promptings of the Spirit. What is the response of the Church? Will Jesus find faithful prayer? Will He once again say,

> *And He saw that there was no man, and wondered that there was no intercessor?*
> ISAIAH 59:16

Jesus is our Intercessor and the High Priest of the New Covenant, yet He calls us to enter into His life and share His labor.

> *For my determined purpose is that I may know Him—that I may progressively become more deeply and intimately acquainted with Him, perceiving and recognizing and understanding the wonders of His Person more strongly, and more clearly. And that I may in that same way come to know the power out-flowing from His resurrection which it exerts over believers; and that I may so share His sufferings as to be continually transformed in spirit into His likeness even to His death.*
> PHILIPPIANS 3:10 AMPLIFIED

What is your response to Jesus' calling?

> *Behold, I stand at the door and knock; if any man hears My voice, and open the door, I will come in to him, and will dine with him, and he with Me. To him that overcomes will I grant to sit with Me in My throne, even as I also overcame and am set down with My Father in His throne. He that has an ear let him hear what the Spirit is saying to the churches.*
> REVELATION 3:20-22

The Essence – God will always find and use an intercessor. It only takes one! One Abraham, one Moses, one Apostle Paul, one John Knox or one Rees Howells; God's eyes are looking throughout the earth to find a human vessel through whom He can do exploits!

two

GOD IS LOOKING – FOR ONE!

THERE IS A CHOSEN GENERATION – a generation of the righteous – a generation that will seek after the Lord and desire to look upon His face (1 Peter 2:8 – 9; Psalm 14:5; 24:6). But in every generation, even in the righteous one, there must be leaders who will stand like lightning rods of faith – who are rooted in Christ's own purity, faith, and integrity. These leaders will be fearless and know their God intimately! They will be men and women given to prayer and to the Word (Acts 6:4). These are those few who will have dared to allow God to set them aside for His Kingdom purposes and plans!

> *And I looked, and, lo, a Lamb stood on the mount Zion, and with Him an hundred forty and four thousand, having His Father's name written in their foreheads.*
>
> REVELATION 14:1

God is on the move! He is searching for Ending Day leaders. God is looking for those who will unreservedly serve Him even to the laying down of their lives. The mark of God upon their lives will be boldness to stand faithful to Christ even upon the pain of death. A boldness to willingly lay down their own wants and plans that His will might have the pre-eminence.

> *And they overcame the devil by the blood of the Lamb, and by the word of their testimony; and they loved not their lives unto the death.*
>
> REVELATION 12:11

> *Then said Jesus unto His disciples, "If any man will come after Me, let him deny himself, and take up his cross, and follow Me."*
>
> MATTHEW 16:24

God is looking for an intercessor through whom His glory can touch the world, and whose prayers will avail much.

And I sought for a man among them, that should make up the hedge, and stand in the gap before Me for the land, that I should not destroy it: but I found none.

EZEKIEL 22:30

The eye of the Lord is looking for the one who will dare believe in spite of the intense pressures and temptations of this life.

For the eyes of the LORD run to and fro throughout the whole earth, to show Himself strong in the behalf of them whose heart is perfect toward Him.

2 CHRONICLES 16:9A

The Lord is looking for one person that He may call and through whom He may complete all His will and counsel. The Lord is looking for one person through whom He can send revival! He is looking for one person through whom He may believe and release revival. He is looking for one person who will be the lightning rod of His glory and thereby impact and change the culture – and the nations!

It only takes one!

And when He had removed Saul, He raised up unto them David to be their king; to whom also He gave testimony, and said, "I have found David the son of Jesse, a man after My own heart, which shall fulfill all My will."

ACTS 13:22

It only takes one!

By faith Noah, being warned of God of things not seen as yet, moved with fear, prepared an ark to the saving of his house; by which he condemned the world, and became heir of the righteousness which is by faith.

HEBREWS 11:7

It only takes one!

It seems one of the greatest trials in life is the test of waiting. King Saul failed this test and it caused his rejection by God and his downfall as king.

Saul waited there seven days for Samuel, as Samuel had instructed him earlier, but Samuel still didn't come. Saul realized that his troops were rapidly slipping away. So he demanded, "Bring me the burnt offering and the peace offerings!" And Saul sacrificed the burnt offering himself. Just as Saul was finishing with the burnt offering, Samuel arrived. Saul went out to meet and welcome him, but Samuel said, "What is this you have done?" Saul replied, "I saw my men scattering from me, and you didn't arrive when you said you would, and the Philistines are at Micmash ready for battle. So I said, 'The Philistines are ready to march against us, and I haven't even asked for the Lord's help!' So I felt obliged to offer the burnt offering myself before you came." "How foolish!" Samuel exclaimed. "You have disobeyed the command of the LORD your God. Had you obeyed, the LORD would have established your kingdom over Israel forever. But now your dynasty must end, for the LORD has sought out a man after His own heart. The LORD has already chosen him to be king over His people, for you have not obeyed the Lord's command."

1 SAMUEL 13:8 – 14 NLT

In your patience possess ye your souls.

LUKE 21:19

It only takes one!

The challenge is to wait despite the fact that all around you pressure is mounting. There are forces, both internal and external, that would compel you to act prematurely and talk foolishly in unbelief. We see this tragically displayed as Jerusalem comes under the brutal siege of the Syrians. When the promise of the Lord's deliverance comes from the prophet of God to the starving city, a high ranking official unwisely speaks out his unbelief.

And while Elisha yet talked with them, behold, the messenger came down unto him: and he said, 'Behold, this evil is of the LORD; what should I wait for the LORD any longer?'...Then Elisha said, "Hear ye the Word of the LORD; 'Thus says the LORD, tomorrow about this time shall a measure of fine flour be sold for a shekel, and two measures of barley for a shekel, in the gate of Samaria.'" Then a lord on whose hand the king leaned answered the man of God, and said, 'Behold, if the LORD would make windows in heaven, might this thing be?' And Elisha said, 'Behold, you shall see it with your eyes, but shall not eat thereof.'

2 KINGS 6:33 & 7:1 – 2

The prophet's words came to pass exactly as he said it would, and while the king's right-hand man saw the Lord's deliverance he didn't live long enough to participate in its blessing! It is a great folly to not wait upon the LORD.

Hear the words of Jesus once again,

In patience you possess your soul.

LUKE 21:19

The writer of Hebrews echoes Jesus when he says,

You have need of patience...

HEBREWS 10:36

And the Psalmist expresses the same thought.

I waited patiently for the LORD; and He inclined unto me, and heard my cry.

PSALM 40:1

Truly my soul waits upon God: from Him comes my salvation. ...My soul, wait only upon God; for my expectation is from Him.

PSALM 62:1, 5

It may try your character severely, but you must learn this truth of patient endurance.

...and having done all, to stand. Stand therefore...

EPHESIANS 6:13C, 14A

It only takes one!
Moses cried out to see God.

And Moses said, "I beseech You, show me Your glory."

EXODUS 33:18

It only takes one!
David openly worshiped at that tabernacle God so fondly remembers as the Tabernacle of David.

My soul longs, yes, even faints for the courts of the LORD: my heart and my flesh cry out for the living God.

PSALM 84:2

And when He had removed him, He raised up unto them David to be their king; to whom also He gave testimony, and said, "I have found David the son of Jesse, a man after My own heart, which shall fulfill all My will." Of this man's seed has God according to his promise raised unto Israel a Saviour, Jesus.

ACTS 13:22 – 23

Will you be the Moses or the David for this generation? Could it be there is an Elijah or Elisha waiting to be unveiled in your mirror?

It only takes one!

Jacob wrestled with God until he possessed the Blessing!

And he said, "I will not let You go, except You bless me."

GENESIS 32:26

Don't give up too soon. Remain steadfast. Hold on with a supernatural tenacity and determination. Remember...

It only takes one!

John Knox's cry for spiritual reality shook his country and impacted the English speaking world! "Give me Scotland lest I die."

It only takes one!

John Hyde, the great apostle of prayer, gave his life in prayer for the masses of India. His desperate prayer, "Give me souls or I die" left a clear and eternal mark on that nation.

It only takes one!

Charles Finney's bold and even audacious prayer challenges us today. "I found myself so much exercised and so borne down with the weight of immortal souls, that I was constrained to pray without ceasing. Some of my experiences indeed alarmed me. A spirit of importunity sometimes came upon me so that I would pray to God that He had made a promise to answer prayer and I could not and would not be denied. I felt so certain that He would hear me that frequently I found myself saying to Him: 'I hope Thou dost not think that I can be denied. I come with Thy faithful promise in my hand, and I can not be denied.' My impression was that the answer was very near, even at the door; and I felt myself strengthened in the Divine life, put on the harness for a mighty conflict with the powers of darkness and expected to see a far more powerful outpouring of the Spirit of God."[1]

It only takes one!

Rees Howells stood as a man uniquely taught of God. His willingness to be wholly surrendered to the Holy Spirit produced fruit and liberty the entire world benefited from as he and the company of intercessors God had given him stood in the gap believing for end of the Nazi regime in Germany. It was in those dark days of the Battle of Britain that Howells asked those assembled with him, "What if millions prayed and no one believed?" From this Spirit inspired challenge they pressed onward and upward in prayer and intercession until the victory was complete. After the war, this same Spirit-chosen company prayed on at the urging of the Lord until the nation of Israel was born in a day! Yes, Rees Howells believed prayer demanded an answer and to this end he gave his life and literally changed the world!

It only takes one.

Could there be a young Peter or John or maybe an aged Paul waiting within your heart to be unleashed from those inner fears or doubting of heart and be used of God to change the world? Could there be a George Whitefield, a John or Charles Wesley or a Charles Finney or another Rees Howells or Dwight Moody waiting to immerge from your home or church to impact the world for Christ?

It only takes one!

And I will restore your judges as at the first, and your counselors as at the beginning: afterward you shall be called, the city of righteousness, the faithful city.

Isaiah 1:26

It only takes one!

If you will persevere in believing prayer you won't be denied. If you will stand fast in faith all things will be made possible for you. If you will hold immovable the promise of God, victory will be yours. If you will remain faithful in your Christian life you will see with your eyes the faithfulness of the Lord.

Yes, yes, yes, a thousand times yes - the Lord will find His intercessors! He will not be denied by men's inabilities or unpredictability. His eyes are looking, even now, throughout the earth to find those human vessels though whom He can do exploits and change the course of history. Will you be one of the faithful persons He finds?

It only takes one!
It only takes one!
It only takes one!

The Essence – As the natural seasons change and flow one to the other, so spiritual seasons change and flow one to another. Prophetic intercession is the heavenly birthed ministry that the Spirit uses to help Him facilitate the changing of spiritual seasons. Using natural means or human vessels, the Lord often gives us a demonstration of clear and vital spiritual truths. Therefore all effective and timely prophetic intercession flows from the heart of the Son of God Himself as He ever lives to make intercession for His people, *three*

THE CHANGING OF THE TIMES AND SEASONS
A LOOK AT PROPHETIC INTERCESSION

And God said, "Let there be lights in the firmament of the heaven to divide the day from the night; and let them be for signs, and for seasons, and for days, and years."

GENESIS 1:14

And He changes the times and the seasons: He removes kings, and sets up kings: He gives wisdom unto the wise, and knowledge to them that know understanding.

DANIEL 2:21

OUR HEAVENLY FATHER, by His sovereign decree, has established an order and sequence of events that govern and rule over the realm of nature as well as the affairs of men.

The Lord has established His throne in the heavens and His Kingdom rules over all.

PSALM 103:19

It is by His good pleasure that the times and seasons have been established. And it is by His good pleasure that they change. He knows the beginning from the end for He is the Beginning and the End.

"I am the Alpha and the Omega," says the LORD God, Who is, and Who was, and Who is to come, the Almighty.

REVELATION 1:8

The prophet Isaiah was allowed to see the root of all prophetic intercession by the Holy Spirit's revelation as he wrote,

Remember this, fix it in mind, take it to heart, you rebels. Remember the former things, those of long ago; I am God, and there is no other; I am God, and there is none like Me. I make known the end from the beginning, from ancient times, what is still to come. I say: My purpose will stand, and I will do all that I please.

ISAIAH 46:8-10

It is from this prayer position that we must begin our understanding of true prophetic intercession – it flows from the predetermined foreknowledge and sovereign decree of the Lord. Prophetic intercession is prayer that joins us with the Chief Intercessor as He manifests His predetermined counsel upon the earth. It is prayer that is totally and utterly dependant upon the Holy Spirit's leading and direction for He alone knows the mind of the Lord and it is He alone who has the ability to reveal that mind to us. Therefore this intercessory ministry must be enabled by the Spirit to see and to hear into the heavenly realms. The key to all prayer, but essential to prophetic intercession, is the moment by moment abiding in Christ necessary to accomplish God's intended purposes through His earthen vessel of the intercessor.

Prophetic intercessions will often display or act out that which is being carried on in the heavenlies. It might be likened to a play that enacts a true to life story only this play is a faith declaration that finds its expression in and is empowered by the Spirit. Elisha instructed the king to take one of his arrows and beat it on the ground when he was faced with a national crisis.

When Elisha was in his last illness, King Jehoash of Israel visited him and wept over him. "My father! My father! The chariots and charioteers of Israel!" he cried. Elisha told him, "Get a bow and some arrows." And the king did as he was told. Then Elisha told the king of Israel to put his hand on the bow, and Elisha laid his own hands on the king's hands. Then he commanded, "Open that eastern window," and he opened it. Then he said, "Shoot!" So he did. Then Elisha proclaimed, "This is the Lord's arrow, full of victory over Aram, for you will completely conquer the Arameans at Aphek. Now pick up the other arrows and strike them against the ground." So the king picked them up and struck the ground three times. But the man of God was angry with him. "You should have struck the ground five or six times!" he exclaimed. "Then you would have beaten Aram until they were entirely destroyed. Now you will be victorious only three times."

2 KING 13:14 – 19

Another example of prophetic intercession is when the Lord instructed the prophet Jeremiah to buy a belt and hide it in the ground near the Euphrates River. As the belt was ruined in the moist earth so the Lord then taught the prophet that pride and idol worship mar the people of God. (Jeremiah 13:1 – 11). Or what of the New Testament prophet Agabus who took the Apostle Paul's belt and acted out a prophetic picture with it? "

And as we were staying there for some days, a certain prophet named Agabus came down from Judea. And coming to us, he took Paul's belt and bound his own feet and hands, and said, "This is what the Holy Spirit says: 'In this way the Jews at Jerusalem will bind the man who owns this belt and deliver him into the hands of the Gentiles.'"

ACTS 21:10 – 11

Times and seasons

Almost everyone has a favorite season or a favorite time of the year. Some of the most spectacular times of the year in Colorado are the changing of the seasons. Winter blooms into spring and brings with it a wonderful freshness and the color of new life. After a long, hot, and dry summer we look forward to Indian Summer, that time in the autumn after the first frost where the days are warm and the nights crisp and clear. It is during this wonderful time of year that the shadows are long and the sun is warm against your skin, while the air is brisk enough for the need to have your jacket handy.

As there are specific seasons within nature, so there are specific seasons within the plan and purposes of the Kingdom of God. The lights in the firmament of the heaven were given to divide not only the day from the night, but they were given to be "for signs, and for seasons, and for days, and years." The seasons within the Kingdom of God, often divide the light of the Gospel from the darkness of the world's system. They provide us with a glimpse into the hearts of specific generations of men and the result of their various attitudes of heart. These examples have been provided that we might apply our hearts to wisdom, learning from those who have preceded us. Jesus even said that certain individuals and generations would be a "sign" for us.

Just as it was in the days of Noah, so also will it be in the days of the Son of Man... it will be just like this on the day the Son of Man is revealed.

Luke 17:26-30

A wicked and adulterous generation seeks after a sign; and there shall no sign be given unto it, but the sign of the prophet Jonah.

Matthew 16:4

How do we come to understand the various seasons within the Kingdom of God? Is it possible to understand the timings of the seasons and if it is, what should be our response? Should our attitude merely be a passive one or are we to take an aggressive posture of prayer and faith concerning the specific seasons in which we find ourselves?

Just before His ascension, the disciples of Jesus asked if he was going to restore the kingdom to Israel. His response was,

It is not for you to know the times or the seasons, which the Father hath put in His own power.

Acts 1:7

Here it seems that knowing of the seasons and times are out of the reach of the believer. Are the seasons beyond our ability to understand or past our finding out? In fact, is that always true? We see Jesus rebuking the religious leaders for wanting a miraculous sign and then challenging them that they don't know how to discern the signs of the times!

You know how to discern the face of the sky; but can you not discern the signs of the times?

Matthew 16:3

And then the Apostle Paul writes to the Thessalonians,

But of the times and seasons, brethren, ye have no need that I write unto you.

1 Thessalonians 5:1

Paul takes it for granted that the saints in Thessalonica are knowledgeable concerning the signs of the times for he continues to write,

But ye brethren, are not in darkness, that that day should overtake you as a thief.

1 Thessalonians 5:5

And again, Jesus cautions that dire consequences may await those that are unaware of the time of their visitation (Luke 19:44). So we can see from the Scriptures that in certain areas concerning the times and seasons, the Lord may simply choose not to inform us (Deuteronomy 29:29). And in other areas we are to have a detailed and an operating knowledge of the seasons for the express purpose that we might act (Daniel 9:2).

In our day of instant weather forecasting, economic forecasting, socio-political forecasting, the plotting of this trend and that trend, there remains a dearth of men who truly understand the times, know what should be done, and can then communicate this to the people with integrity of heart and character. An anemic life of prayer is not enough for us to grasp hold of the events of today. No matter how well informed and accurate they may be, learned and religious men even with all of their plots, graphs and trends are not enough to help us face our troubled times. It is time for godly men to lay hold of eternal things, to obtain heavenly answers for earthly problems, and by the Spirit of God break out of the realm of the natural and flow into that realm inhabited by the Victorious One, the Ancient of Days, the LORD of Glory! It is here in the realm of prophetic intercession that the Lord begins to reveal His mind and His thoughts. It is here that He invites us to join with Him in His intercession to transform and change the times and seasons.

Prophetic intercession is prayer that joins us with the Chief Intercessor as He manifests His predetermined counsel upon the earth. It is at His bidding and word that the change of the times and the seasons transpire.

And He changes the times and the seasons: He removes kings, and sets up kings: He gives wisdom unto the wise, and knowledge to them that know understanding.

Daniel 2:21

It is as the Lord unites our hearts with His in intercession that we become partakers of His labor in prayer. Prophetic intercession is prayer that merely walks out the works foreordained of the Lord, releasing from simple actions (and sometimes seemingly foolish acts) great spiritual truths and power into the natural realm.

For we are His workmanship, created in Christ Jesus unto good works, which God hath before ordained that we should walk in them.
EPHESIANS 2:10

In the Old Testament we see prophetic intercession and action as the Lord calls Isaiah to declare what was coming upon the nation of Israel by the very names he was to give his children, or how Jeremiah was instructed not to marry as a sign of the Lord's dealings with Israel, or Hosea's call to marry Gomer, the prostitute, or the many peculiar acts of Ezekiel. In the New Testament, we again see similar prophetic acts as Agabus prophesies of the Apostle Paul's coming imprisonment in Jerusalem.

Prophetic intercession is a heavenly ministry. It is a ministry birthed in heaven, fought in the heavenlies, and finally, demonstrated upon the earth. Prophetic intercession issues from the very depths of Heaven itself as the Lord Jesus Christ calls the intercessor into His presence and heart. Effective intercession flows from the heart of the Son of God Himself as He ever lives to make intercession for His people,

Wherefore He is able also to save them to the uttermost that come unto God by Him, seeing He ever lives to make intercession for them.
HEBREWS 7:25

Intercessions' work may appear to be quietly done within the prayer closet, but in reality it is intense labor within the heavenly realm.

For we do not wrestle against flesh and blood, but against principalities, against powers, against the rulers of the darkness of this age, against spiritual hosts of wickedness in the heavenly places.
EPHESIANS 6:12

Of necessity, intercession must operate within the heavenly realm. It is in this spiritual realm where Jesus calls us to make our stand. It is here with Him in the yoke of intercession and prophetic release we experience His sure importunity and divinely empowered patience which fuels along our lives of hidden prayer in Him. Such is the intercessor who along with Christ sees the sinful and needy hearts of men turned to a loving heavenly Father.

It is true that I am an ordinary, weak human being, but I don't use human plans and methods to win my battles. I use God's mighty

weapons, not those made by men, to knock down the devils strongholds. These weapons can break down every proud argument against God and every wall that can be built to keep men from finding Him. With these weapons I can capture rebels and bring them back to God, and change them into men whose hearts' desire is obedience to Christ.

2 CORINTHIANS 10:3-5 LIVING

It is here in this yoke of ministry with Jesus that men's eyes are opened and their hearts are softened to the complete and finished sacrifice of the Messiah.

For the intercession of the Lord Jesus Christ to be birthed within our hearts, we must take the time to wait upon the Lord and minister unto Him.

As they ministered to the Lord and fasted, the Holy Spirit said...

ACTS 13:2

I was in the Spirit on the Lord's Day, and I heard behind me a loud voice, as of a trumpet saying...

REVELATION 1:10-11

It is as we wait upon the Lord that He speaks to us and makes known the revelation of His plans and purposes. As the Holy Spirit begins to make known the heart of the Father to us, we are awakened to the needs of those around us. It is here, in the presence of the Lord that the seed of intercession is planted. As more of the character of the Lord Jesus is formed within us, the more we begin to understand His burden and compassion upon the lost and dying.

As this seed of intercession grows within our hearts and as we yield to its promptings, great power begins to be released through our prayers. It is within this place of agreement with the Chief Intercessor Himself, the Lord Jesus, that the secret of the intercessor's power in prayer is found.

Intercession is successfully fought in the heavenlies as we yield to the working of the Holy Spirit and come to a place of complete abiding in the Son.

If you abide in Me, and My words abide in you, you will ask what you desire, and it shall be done for you.

JOHN 15:7

It is here in this place of abiding within the life and resurrection power of the Lord Jesus that our prayer of intercession takes on the dynamic of victorious, triumphant, and overcoming authority. Because intercession is clearly the ministry of the Lord Jesus Christ, it is His faith and His prayer of intercession that must be released through the intercessor! For this reason the intercessor must of necessity be yielded to the workings and leadings of the Holy Spirit. The life of the intercessor must be free of his own agendas, desires, preconceived notions and ideas. A life that has been crucified with Jesus is of utmost importance if the Lord is to live His life of intercession out through that individual's life.

> *I have been crucified with Christ; it is not longer I who live, but Christ lives in me; and the life which I now live in the flesh I live by the faith of the Son of God, who loved me and gave Himself for me.*
> GALATIANS 2:20

It is the crucified life that is of the highest value to the Holy Spirit in this work and ministry of intercession. The one who has died to self and has,

> *...prepared himself as a vessel of honor will be sanctified and fit for the Master's use; prepared for every good work.*
> 2 TIMOTHY 2:21

It is often said of the intercessor that he carries the "burden of the Lord." While this may be true, we must also note that the burden of the Lord is light and that His yoke is easy (Matthew 11:30). When intercession becomes only a heavy burden and a joyless load to carry, this is often evidence that the "burden" is no longer being carried by the Lord but by the individual. And at this point we must examine ourselves to see if in fact the burden we are carrying has been received by the Lord or is of our own workings and imaginings. The loss of joyful anticipation and confident expectation concerning a specific intercession can be an effective barometer concerning the validity of a heavenly prayer burden. When we are in the yoke with the Lord, His presence provides all the joy, strength, and encouragement we need to sustain us until the answer comes (See Psalm 16:11; Nehemiah 8:10; John 16:20-24). So, it is the Lord Jesus Christ living His life in us and through us that is the hope of our victory and power in intercession.

> *...Christ in you, the hope of glory.*
> COLOSSIANS 1:27

Without His life flow within us, we come to the end of our own human strength and stamina all too quickly. It is His inexhaustible supply that we draw from and rely upon. As we intercede with the intercessory burden of Jesus, we are in a place to exchange strength with Him, thereby receiving His grace and power for the task at hand.

Hast thou not known? Hast thou not heard that the everlasting God, the LORD, the Creator of the ends of the earth, faints not, neither is weary? There is no searching of His understanding. He gives power to the faint; and to them that have no might He increases strength. Even the youths shall faint and be weary, and the young men shall utterly fall, but they that wait upon the LORD shall renew (exchange) their strength; they shall mount up with wings like eagles; they shall run, and not be weary; and they shall walk, and not faint.

ISAIAH 40:28-31

It is here within this place of total dependence upon the Lord for our very life's strength that we can draw near to the One who has been touched with the feeling of our own infirmities, and was tempted like we have been, yet without sin. It is before this One that we can boldly come to obtain mercy, and find grace to help in time of need (Hebrews 4:15-16). As He has entered into our lives experiencing every joy and sorrow, successfully facing every temptation, so He calls us into His intercessory life where there is sufficient grace and mercy to meet every need. It is here that there is no lack of strength, compassion or power. It is from this position in Christ that victory is continuously experienced. The answer of intercession is demonstrated to the world as we humble ourselves and begin to act upon the Lord's Word that has come through the specific intercession.

Elijah was man subject to like passions as we are, and he prayed earnestly that it might not rain; and it rained not on the earth by the space of three years and six months. And he prayed again, and the heaven gave rain, and the earth brought forth her fruit.

JAMES 5:17-18

Time spent in prayer without a willingness to be the answer yourself or by then enacting the corresponding faith responses and conduct are ultimately just empty and idle words. Our willingness to be the answer, or at least to be a part of the answer, is a key to the Holy Spirit releasing His intercessory authority through our prayer.

If ye be willing and obedient, ye shall eat the good of the land.

ISAIAH 1:19

The good of the land, the answer to the intercession, is promised to the willing. As we willingly pick up the cross that the Lord Jesus calls us to bear, not only do we become identified with Him in name, but we become His disciples and we begin to become identified with His sufferings as well.

If any man will come after Me, let him deny himself, and take up his cross, and follow Me.

MATTHEW 16:24

That I may know Him, and the power of His resurrection, and the fellowship of His sufferings, being made conformable unto His death.

PHILIPPIANS 3:10

It is within this willingness to follow Jesus into His sufferings, at whatever the cost, that enables the intercessor to obtain the desired end (see Hebrews 12:2).

Willingness, however, is not all that is required. Obedience is just as vital to our place of intercession. Jesus, the Perfect Mediator and Intercessor, walked out the perfect intercession by His obedience to the Father's command.

Who in the days of His flesh, when He had offered up prayers and supplications with strong crying and tears unto Him that was able to save Him from death, and was heard in that He feared; though He were a Son, yet learned He obedience by the things which He suffered; and being made perfect, He became the author of eternal salvation unto all them that obey Him.

HEBREWS 5:7-9

Jesus' obedience was complete as He humbled Himself and became obedient unto death, even the death of the cross. (Philippians 2:8). Our words may declare our intentions, but it is our obedient actions that declare our genuine faith!

But what do you think? A certain man had two sons; and he came to the first, and said, "Son, go work today in my vineyard." He answered and said, "I will not"; but afterward he repented, and went. And he came to the second, and said the same. And he answered and said, "I go, sir"; and went not. Which of the two did the will of the father?

Matthew 21:28-30

And so it is with intercession. Our willingness of attitude, united with our obedient compliance to the requests of the Spirit release great joy in Heaven and answers into the earth. These principles are always immeasurably linked together and they must be exercised together if we are to stand up to the full measure of the Divine Intercessor, the Lord Jesus Christ.

As Jesus walked out His full and complete intercession upon the earth, willing not only to be fully man, but to submit to death that had no legal right to Him, so He calls us to live out the life of intercession with Him.

As My Father has sent Me, even so send I you.

John 20:21

The Scriptures are clear that there is one, and only one Burden Bearer, yet this One still calls us into ministry with Him to carry the burdens of others.

Bear one another's burdens, and so fulfill the law of Christ.

Galatians 6:2

And you will be called priests of the LORD, and you will be named ministers of our God.

Isaiah 61:6

And again,

You also, like living stones, are being built into a spiritual house to be a holy priesthood, offering spiritual sacrifices acceptable to God through Jesus Christ... But you are a chosen people, a royal priesthood, a holy nation, a people belonging to God, that you may declare the praises of Him who called you out of darkness into His wonderful light.

1 Peter 2:5,9

Our Lord, being a prophetic God, demonstrates prophetic intercession by first declaring the coming of Messiah and then by Messiah's coming to live out and become the very redemption which He prophesied from the beginning (i.e. Genesis 3:15; Isaiah 7:14; Isaiah 53). And so it is within our own lives, every event prepares us for the next all under the Father's sovereign superintending care. It is from this preparation and then experiential understanding that the Lord begins to develop our trust and expectation in Him, and then our confidence in His purposes, as we see His hand move and bring about the intercession to which He has called us.

Our Lord is a God of perfect timing. It is He that has ordered and established the universe, its very rhythm, the one He has orchestrated. The coming of the Redeemer was at the perfect time, not a moment too soon, not a moment too late.

But when the fullness of the time was come, God sent forth His Son, made of a woman, made under the law. To redeem them that were under the law, that we might receive the adoption of sons.
GALATIANS 4:4-5

That in the dispensation of the fullness of times He might gather together in one all things in Christ, both which are in heaven, and which are on earth; even in Him...
EPHESIANS 1:10

John Wesley said, "God will do nothing, but in answer to prayer." The prophet Ezekiel said,

And I sought for a man among them, that should make up the hedge, and stand in the gap before Me for the land, that I should not destroy it...
EZEKIEL 22:30

The Lord is looking for willing partners who will purpose to share this burden with Him and begin to enter into His intercession. As the seasons of the spiritual realm begin to change, the Lord begins to speak to the hearts of those that have drawn near to Him, and He begins to reveal His purposes and plan.

Surely the Lord God will do nothing, but He reveals His secret unto His servants the prophets.
AMOS 3:7

As the Lord came to judge the cities of Sodom and Gomorrah, His response concerning Abraham was,

Shall I hide from Abraham what I am about to do?

GENESIS 18:17

And even the coming of Jesus had not gone unnoticed by those who had previously drawn near to the Lord's heart. Like Simeon, who had been...

waiting for the consolation of Israel, and the Holy Spirit was upon him, and it was revealed unto him by the Holy Spirit, that he should not see death, before he had seen the Lord's Christ, And he came into the temple by the Holy Spirit... then he took Him (the baby Jesus) up in his arms, and blessed God, and said, "Lord, now let Thy servant depart in peace, according to Thy Word; for my eyes have seen Thy salvation."

LUKE 2:25-32

Simeon, had spent years walking intimately with the Lord. His relationship was such with the Lord that the Lord not only revealed the times, but even the way of His salvation. It is this kind of men and women that must come forth in these last moments of history; men who out of an intimate relationship with God, are moved by the Spirit of God according to the Word of God. It is these people, like Simeon of old, who will see manifest the purpose of God in this hour.

No doubt the Voice of the Lord is speaking to His people in this moment of time. The question we must face is, "Is anyone listening?" Are your ears tuned to the voice of the Spirit? Would you heed His voice if you heard it? Have you made yourself available to respond to His calling? Are you willing to obey and to follow Him wherever He goes? Selah.

The Essence – As certain police motorcycles may lead a parade or motorcade, there are certain individuals, and at times, even companies of believers who are called of God to be forerunners or the vanguard of His Spirit's moving throughout the earth. These humble servants of the Lord are often acting as prophetic intercessors, and are themselves unaware of their unique calling in God, but through their lives and ministries they are acting as both servants and examples to the greater Body of Christ that something big is about ready to arrive on the scene.

four

OF MOTORCYCLES AND DONKEYS

But God hath chosen the foolish things of the world to confound the wise.

1 CORINTHIANS 1:27A

JUST AS IT IS HELPFUL to know our own personal and family medical histories, so, as Christians it can be helpful for us to understand our personal, corporate, and spiritual DNA. At work we understand that it is important for us to have an accurate job description so that we can perform to our employer's expectations. As it is essential to know these natural things so it is vital for us to understand our spiritual makeup and the specific assignment(s) given to us by the Spirit of God if we are to "run our race" with accuracy and determination to a specific end. Every believer has been given uniquely tailored giftings that will enable them to fulfill the call of God upon their lives as well as assist and call others to their divinely appointed tasks for the Kingdom!

The prophetic and intercessory ministries of the Church have been given to us by the resurrected Christ (Ephesians 4). They have been given to the end that we may be the people of God walking through the earth in the manner worthy and pleasing to Him. These gifts have also been given so that we may carry the power and accuracy necessary to proclaim the Gospel to the ends of the earth.

The Scriptures are full of pictures and analogies that reveal to us the many facets of the Kingdom. They also are full of keys that will unleash the power and attestation of the Kingdom to an unbelieving world. The Bible is also full of natural images that reveal to us deeper spiritual truths. Jesus' method of teaching was most often the use of parables. Through these natural pictures and stories He related eternal truths to the people as well as to His disciples. As we look at motorcycles and donkeys we'll

Mark D. Spencer

discover important implications that will help us better live victorious and powerful Christian lives. Let's see then what motorcycles and donkeys can teach us about eternal things.

> *Howbeit that was not first which is spiritual, but that which is natural; and afterward that which is spiritual.*
>
> 1 CORINTHIANS 15:46

What is this of donkeys?

The donkey is an odd, yet determined little animal. The donkey is well adapted to desert climates as well as mountainous terrain, making it a perfect beast of burden. The donkey is often the brunt of jokes and is seen as one of the lowliest animals in the barnyard. The character of a donkey or burro is typically stubborn and fiercely self-willed. To hurl an insult at someone, especially someone who is themselves stubborn or set in their ways is to call them a donkey – or worse! Though not as regal or as powerful as its larger cousin the horse, the donkey finds himself playing key roles throughout the Scriptures. From Saul's lost donkeys that ultimately led him to the prophet of God – the very prophet that would anoint him as King of Israel – to Balaam's talking donkey and to the young donkey called upon to carry the King of kings on His prophetic and triumphant entry into Jerusalem, the humble donkey has something to teach the modern day Church.

The ministry of the donkey

Yes, even a donkey can have a ministry! No matter who you are, no matter where you are from, no matter what you have done; the Spirit of God has a ministry set aside for you. Redemption reaches deep within the very heart and soul of man, transforming him and setting him on a course in life and that life is intended to be overflowing with blessing.

> *Now there are diversities of gifts, but the same Spirit. And there are differences of administrations, but the same Lord. And there are diversities of operations, but it is the same God which works all in all. But the manifestation of the Spirit is given to every man to profit thereby.*
>
> 1 CORINTHIANS 12:4 – 7

A prophet to the prophet

Now then, no matter what estimation you may hold concerning yourself, God is surely able to anoint, even you, for His specific purposes – if you'll yield to His Spirit! If Balaam's donkey could become a prophet to the prophet, what might God do with your life once yielded to His Divine craftsmanship?

> *And Balaam rose up in the morning, and saddled his ass, and went with the princes of Moab. And God's anger was kindled because he went: and the angel of the LORD stood in the way as an adversary against him. ... And the ass saw the angel of the LORD standing in the way, and his sword drawn in his hand... And the LORD opened the mouth of the ass, and she said unto Balaam, 'What have I done unto you, that you hast hit me these three times?' And Balaam said unto the ass, 'Because you have mocked me if I had a sword in my hand I would kill you.' And the ass said unto Balaam, 'Am not I your ass, upon which you have ridden ever since I was yours unto this day? Have I ever done anything like this to you before?' And he said, 'Nay.' Then the LORD opened the eyes of Balaam, and he saw the angel of the LORD standing in the way, and his sword drawn in his hand: and he bowed down his head, and fell flat on his face.*
>
> NUMBERS 22:21 – 34

Imagine, an adult, a prophet no less, who has had numerous supernatural dealings, standing in the middle of a road having an argument with a donkey!? And he is totally oblivious to the angelic presence standing with drawn sword in front of him! Balaam's greed coupled with the internal spiritual forces of anger and frustration blinded him to the genuine presence and glory of God. How often have you missed the glory and wonder of God's presence because you were acting and moving in a negative, soulish or even hateful way? Could it be that the Lord has used an employer or teacher, parent or neighbor in an attempt to speak into your life and yet you were self-blinded to what should have been the spiritually obvious? Could those accidents or various other troubles and trials be attempting to warn you of your continued and ongoing disobedience? Could it be that your disregard for the things of the Kingdom has caused you to become so dull of hearing that the once clear voice of the Master has become dulled. Could it be that you are now suffering the consequences of those disobediences and actions? And yet, like a stubborn donkey, you still refuse to hear or obey!

Selah – Stop and think on that.

Still, the miracle of a talking donkey is beckoning to us. It is far more than a fairly tale. It is the Creator in His great love for His people, as well as for the misguided prophet, reaching out through whatever means is necessary to offer them a life-giving word – if they – if Balaam – if you – will only turn a listening and attentive ear!

Surely Balaam and his donkey serve as examples for us to learn many lessons. But in this moment another lesson for us to grasp is that if a donkey can become the mouthpiece of the Creator God, then most surely, you and I can be anointed and used of the same God to speak His life transforming Gospel to those around us!

> *I am the LORD your God, which brought you out of the land of Egypt open your mouth wide, and I will fill it. But My people would not hearken to My voice; and Israel would not listen to Me. So I gave them up to their own hearts' lust and they walked in their own counsels. Oh that My people would have hearkened unto Me, and that Israel had walked in My ways! I should soon have subdued their enemies, and turned My hand against their adversaries.*
>
> PSALM 81:10 – 14

Don't be like those who refuse! Don't yield to the fears and anxieties or the myriad of psychosis, inferiority complexes, or shyness (which are but excuses to not obey the Great Commission of Jesus Christ). But rather boldly confess and receive that "spirit of power, and of love and of a sound mind" promised us (2 Timothy 1:7).

Jesus said that in a moment of need if we would only rely upon the indwelling Holy Spirit, we would experience His manifest presence both within and upon us – enabling us to speak His Word to the circumstance!

> *But when they shall lead you, and deliver you up, take no thought beforehand what you shall speak, neither do you need to premeditate but whatsoever shall be given you in that hour, that speak for it is not you that speaks, but the Holy Ghost.*
>
> MARK 13:11

It is a faith proposition for sure! But don't be afraid. As you walk through your day praying in the Holy Spirit, meditating upon the Word of God, walking in the love of God, you will be more than ready, in an instant, to become the oracle of God. Release your faith in God's ability in you.

If any man speak, let him speak as the oracles of God.

1 PETER 4:11

A limousine for the Christ

Moving from talking donkeys to the life of Christ, we see how another donkey, a borrowed donkey, maybe even a distant relative of Balaam's donkey, now becomes the vehicle of one of Messiah's most significant prophetic actions. Jesus makes a bold declaration to the House of Israel. He enters the ancient city of Jerusalem "lowly, and riding upon an ass." Yet in this humble posture His command presence still captivates the city and its people. But beyond the prophetic action, which is pointing to that Day of His Second Advent, He also declares prophetically the destiny of the nations! Let's listen as we hear Messiah's blessings and judgments that were decreed during this moment of prophetic timing – and all from the back of a humble donkey...

Rejoice greatly, O daughter of Zion; shout, O daughter of Jerusalem behold, your King comes unto you He is just, and having salvation; lowly, and riding upon an ass, and upon a colt the foal of an ass... And I will cut off the chariot from Ephraim, and the horse from Jerusalem, and the battle bow shall be cut off and He shall speak peace unto the heathen and His dominion shall be from sea even to sea, and from the river even to the ends of the earth... And the LORD shall be seen over them, and His arrow shall go forth as the lightning and the Lord GOD shall blow the trumpet, and shall go with whirlwinds of the south... And the LORD their God shall save them in that day as the flock of His people for they shall be as the stones of a crown, lifted up as an ensign upon His land. For how great is His goodness, and how great is His beauty! Corn shall make the young men cheerful, and new wine the maids.

ZECHARIAH 9:9-17

Most surely it will come to pass! Prophetic actions which portend the future's actuality will often appear as foolishness to those upon whom their significance is lost! Imagine what the on-looking Roman soldiers must have thought as they saw this Jewish Rabbi riding on a little donkey with the crowds crying "Hosanna, Blessed is He Who comes in the name of the LORD!" These hardened soldiers who had seen their Caesar processing in Rome upon a brilliant white and magnificently groomed stallion, surrounded by legions of Rome's finest, battle hardened soldiers, must surely have chuckled if not laughed out loud! Maybe some of them even thought that it was some sort of Jewish festival and the people were mocking and lampooning their hated, national betrayer, King Herod. All such prophetic pictures acted out are not for the fool but rather for the one who will believe. And so is the imagery of this prophetic action – God using a foolish, natural thing to offer a picture of a coming Age and Kingdom along with its King! This simple prophetic action may have been upon a little burro, but Messiah will return upon His charger and on that day no one will be laughing! It's a true saying, "He ain't coming back to preach!"[2]

> *And I saw heaven opened, and behold a white horse; and He that sat upon him was called Faithful and True, and in righteousness He does judge and make war. His eyes were as a flame of fire, and on His head were many crowns; and He had a name written, that no man knew, but He Himself. And He was clothed with a vesture dipped in blood and His name is called The Word of God. And the armies which were in heaven followed Him upon white horses, clothed in fine linen, white and clean. And out of His mouth goes a sharp sword, that with it He should smite the nations and He shall rule them with a rod of iron and He treads the winepress of the fierceness and wrath of Almighty God.*
>
> REVELATION 19:11 – 15

The wisdom of the donkey

This little donkey had never been sat upon. He had not yet been tamed of men. Yet, there was no resistance given, no rebellion offered. At the Master's initial touch, this colt yielded his will, surrendered his self-determination, and fully submitted to the Master's will.

> *As they came to the towns of Bethphage and Bethany, on the Mount of Olives, He sent two disciples ahead. "Go into that village over there," He told them, "and as you enter it, you will see a colt tied there that has never been ridden. Untie it and bring it here. If anyone asks what you are doing, just say, 'The Lord needs it.'" ...So they brought the colt to Jesus and threw their garments over it for Him to ride on. Then the crowds spread out their coats on the road ahead of Jesus.*
>
> LUKE 19:29 – 44 NLT

Okay, I see that even a donkey in the Master's hands can have a ministry and yet, it does seem a little peculiar, doesn't it? Exactly what is this "ministry"? It seems we have often misunderstood the meaning of ministry. Ministry is not merely something that professionals do. It is not some super spiritual act or a ceremony conducted by those appointed to head a specific church or denomination. Ministry can be that act of service, or that act of kindness offered in Jesus' name to those in need. Ministry is simply allowing Jesus to bless and care for others through us by creating within us desires and abilities and actions that touch other's lives! To strive for a place of ministry is to reach for the wrong thing.

Then the mother of Zebedee's children, along with her sons James and John, came worshipping Him, and desiring a certain thing of Him. And He said unto her, "What do you want?" And she said unto Him, "Grant that my two sons may sit, the one on Your right hand, and the other on the left, in Your Kingdom." But Jesus answered and said, "You don't know what you're asking. Are ye able to drink of the cup that I shall drink of, and to be baptized with the baptism that I am baptized with?" They say unto him, "We are able." And He said unto them, "You shall drink indeed of My cup, and be baptized with the baptism that I am baptized with: but to sit on My right hand, and on My left, is not Mine to give, but it shall be given to them for whom it is prepared of My Father." And when the ten other disciples heard it, they were moved with indignation against the two brethren. But Jesus called them unto Himself, and said, "You know that the princes of the Gentiles exercise dominion over them, and they that are great exercise authority over them. But it shall not be so among you: but whosoever will be great among you, let him be your minister; and whosoever will be chief among you, let him be your servant: Even as the Son of man came not to be ministered unto, but to minister, and to give His life a ransom for many."

MATTHEW 20:20-28

That's right! Our primary ministry, like the donkey's is to be a servant. We are called to be burden bearers. We are called to bear the weight of others. We are called to willingly serve at those assignments that no one else will do or even desire to do.

Bear one another's burdens, and so fulfill the law of Christ.

GALATIANS 6:2

Mark D. Spencer

The donkey's purpose

A life lived without purpose is arguably not a life at all. The Creator's intent for His people is to live life to the full (John 10:10). Life is meant to be full!

And God blessed them, and God said unto them, "Be fruitful, and multiply, and replenish the earth, and subdue it: and have dominion over the fish of the sea, and over the fowl of the air, and over every living thing that moves upon the earth."

GENESIS 1:28

Every believer has a God-given and God-ordained purpose for living.

The donkey's first job was to carry Jesus. He was to get Him where He needed to go safely and surely. As Jesus came into Jerusalem to fulfill the divine plan of God, so He also wants to gain access into the arena of your life to the same end. An arena is defined as an open space of ground, specifically where gladiators in ancient Rome exhibited their skills of hand to hand combat. Therefore an arena is a place of public exhibition. Jesus wants to so live His live through you so as to gain access to all of those people around you who are in need of His forgiveness and grace. Wherever we find people, whether in your family home or in an apartment complex or surrounding neighborhood; whether you find them in the work place, school or university; maybe you'll find them in the market place or in the park; the Spirit can use you and wants to use you to impact them for Christ's sake.

We can see the donkey as a type or picture of that which allows Jesus to enter our lives, our ministries and our businesses with His Kingdom and thereby gain an entrance into the lives of those who are within the sphere of our influence.

Our purpose... blessed to be a blessing!

When Jesus has gained an entrance into your life certain things will begin to change.

And when He was come into Jerusalem, all the city was moved, saying, "Who is this?" And the multitude said, "This is Jesus the prophet of Nazareth of Galilee." And Jesus went into the temple of God, and cast out all them that sold and bought in the temple, and overthrew the tables of the moneychangers, and the seats of them that sold doves, and said unto them, "It is written, My house shall be called the house of prayer; but you have made it a den of thieves." And the blind and the lame came to Him in the temple; and He healed them. And when the chief priests and scribes saw the wonderful things that He did, and the children crying in the temple, and saying, "Hosanna to the son of David" they were very displeased, and they said unto him, "Do You hear what these are saying?" And Jesus said to them, "Yes, have you never read, 'Out of the mouth of babes and children You have perfected praise?'" And He left them...

MATTHEW 21:10 – 17

Let's see if we can glean from this passage of Scripture what to expect when Jesus comes riding into our lives. There will be a confrontation with you one way or another – it is inevitable (Vs 10). He will judge any sin that is in your life. He will begin to create within you a life of prayer (Vs 13). He will bring great blessing – if you only will come to Him (Vs 14). The hearts of the rebellious will be hardened (Vs 15). And He will produce "a new song of praise in your heart" (Vs 15 – 16).

After He impacts you, He will then allow you; no He will then expect you to impact the lives of others! We are called to use our influence with others for His purposes and His glory. It is His plan, and He has no intention of changing His mind (Malachi 3:6). "Be fruitful and multiply," those words spoken in the Garden are still operative and the divine demand and command is still upon the saint of God. With this in mind, what would you say is your purpose in ministry?

Your purpose – that is, your ministry, your money, your time, and yes, even your life are intended to give Jesus the opportunity to make you into a public exhibition of His goodness and redemption! People are looking at you all the time. And they are making judgments and opinions constantly. We are to be light. We are to be salt. We are to become, to the peoples of the world, both a symbol and a source of blessing – God's blessing.

Among the nations, Judah and Israel had become symbols of what it means to be cursed. But no longer! Now I will rescue you and make you both a symbol and a source of blessing! So don't be afraid or discouraged, but instead get on with rebuilding the Temple!

ZECHARIAH 8:13 NLT

Mark D. Spencer

Is your present life – in any area – causing those within the world's system to hunger and thirst after our God? Of what are you a symbol? And is your life a source of blessing to others? Shouldn't we be making the world jealous for our Christ?

> *But I say, did not Israel know? First Moses said, "I will provoke you to jealousy by them that are no people, and by a foolish nation I will anger you."*
> ROMAN 10:19

Still in force...

This is the ancient blessing that is still in covenant force—

> *...and I will bless you and make your name great; and you shall be a blessing, and I will bless them that bless you, and curse him that curses you, and in you shall all families of the earth be blessed.*
> GENESIS 12:2B – 3

We have been blessed to be a blessing! It is God who has empowered His people from within! He has vested Himself into His people to the end that we might be witnesses to the Gospel in power and demonstration!

> *But you shall receive power, after that the Holy Ghost is come upon you and you shall be witnesses unto Me both in Jerusalem, and in all Judaea, and in Samaria, and unto the uttermost part of the earth.*
> ACTS 1:8

> *And my speech and my preaching was not with enticing words of man's wisdom, but in demonstration of the Spirit and of power, that your faith should not stand in the wisdom of men, but in the power of God.*
> 1 CORINTHIANS 2:4 – 5

It is plain – the witness of the Gospel is to be offered in both word and in power. Signs and wonders are to follow the believer's life. Signs and wonders are to follow you!

> *And they went forth, and preached everywhere, the Lord working with them, and confirming the Word with signs following. Amen.*
> MARK 16:20

Are you willing...?

Now, the Greek word for witness also means to be a martyr! Though thousands have died for their faith in Christ, relatively few of us will have the opportunity to do so. Still, every believer is called upon and is given the opportunity to live life as a living martyr!

I am crucified with Christ, nevertheless I live, yet not I, but Christ lives in me, and the life I live in the flesh I live by the faith of the Son of God who loved me and gave Himself for me.

GALATIANS 2:20

Our overcoming is linked with our testimony of Jesus' work within us as well as our willingness to die to self.

And they overcame Satan by the blood of the Lamb, and by the word of their testimony; and they loved not their lives unto the death.

REVELATION 12:11

We are to bear within our lives a love so great, a love so pure, that we live our lives wholly to the Christ, dying to our own selfish interests and motives, living unto Him and for Him! It is the martyr's call to lay down our own selfish natures that we may "know Jesus and make Him known." And it is from that internal empowering that enables us to take Jesus into every man's world!

Then said Jesus unto His disciples, "If any man will come after Me, let him deny himself, and take up his cross, and follow Me. For whosoever will save his life shall lose it and whosoever will lose his life for My sake shall find it. For what is a man profited, if he shall gain the whole world, and lose his own soul? or what shall a man give in exchange for his soul?

MATTHEW 16:24 – 26

Are we willing to be donkeys for Christ by our willingness to serve others and bear the burdens that others carry? As 'donkeys' shouldn't we serve quietly without clamoring for the recognition of men that rather than seeing us they might see Jesus? As 'donkeys' shouldn't we serve without demand of reciprocation? As 'donkeys' shouldn't we serve others without the internal drive to explain ourselves, advance ourselves, or defend ourselves?

Mark D. Spencer

I must decrease, but He must increase.

JOHN 3:30

Three little questions...

A monk from the Trappist tradition challenges us with this brief but intensely revealing and personal evaluation. Ask yourself these three questions, "Am I willing to not be esteemed? I am I willing to not be in control?" And finally, "Am I willing not to be secure?" These deeply longed for, yet on many levels, intangible things, are really only ever found in Christ. To be esteemed by God is to hear the ultimate affirmation as we one day hear these words of Jesus,

> *"Well done, good and faithful servant; thou hast been faithful over a few things, I will make thee ruler over many things: enter thou into the joy of thy Lord.!"*

MATTHEW 25:23

To let go of our control is to trust Him completely and live a life yielded to Him Who holds all things together by the Word of His power!

> *Who being the brightness of His glory, and the express image of His person, and upholding all things by the Word of His power...*

HEBREWS 1:3

To be genuinely secure is to walk with Him Who is Himself our "Shield and exceedingly great Reward" (Genesis 15:1).

These three questions penetrate our defenses and force us to squarely face the issues of our true spirituality, all the while, revealing our true character. They reach deep into the recesses of our personality, they probe for hidden fears and insecurities, they invite us to begin the heart revealing process of why we have such a great need to constantly defend our motives and actions – and such responses always uncover those areas we thought were once fully surrendered to Jesus.

Are you willing to not be esteemed?

Are you willing to not be in control?

Are you willing to not be secure?

The donkey's occupation – a beast of burden.

Bear ye one another's burdens, and so fulfill the law of Christ.
GALATIANS 6:2

How prestigious it must have been to carry the Christ – the King of
Israel! But lest we forget, the primary vocation of the donkey is as a beast
of burden. Now you may argue, "It's not my responsibility to carry other
people's loads." But if we carry Christ, isn't that the very meaning of being
a Christian? One who carries the Christ? Or one who is like Christ – a
little Christ? And isn't it His nature now within you to bear the burden
of others? It is as natural for the Christian to reach out to the burdened
as it is for a donkey to carry a heavy load. Yes, the believer is called to be
a "beast of burden." You are called to be a burden bearer.

Bear ye one another's burdens, and so fulfill the law of Christ.
GALATIANS 6:2

Burden bearing is the royal law of love in action (James 2:8). Burden
bearing is tough work. Not only is the act of bearing another's burdens
challenging enough, but we then must also learn to cast the care of that
burden upon the Lord, for He alone is the true and ultimate Burden
Bearer! But there are other challenges that await the Christian "donkey".
It is all too easy when praying for others, empathizing with others, or
serving others to miss our own God-given calling. Hear the Lord's
warning to all who would carry others burdens...

*Issachar is a strong donkey, lying down between the sheepfolds. When he
saw that a resting place was good and that the land was pleasant, He
bowed his shoulder to bear burdens, and became a slave at forced labor.*
GENESIS 49:14-15 NASB

Now Issachar, even though renowned for having prophetic wisdom (1
Chronicles 12:32), fell prey to the easiness of merely serving – no need to
be on the edge, no need to stay before the Lord in prayer, no need to be a
bold witness evangelistically, or to speak out prophetically. It is easier to
let somebody else make all the decisions and take the brunt of the heat for
having made the tough decisions. It's easy to say, "As long as I'm serving
or bearing burdens I won't be persecuted or misunderstood." Issachar
so fell into this trap that the tribe became slaves to others. It is easy for
a genuine servant to abdicate their own personal responsibilities and

simply bear the burdens of others. Rather than face the personal burdens of bearing those private responsibilities. However, you are never really relieved from them, but rather only have the sensations of being relieved from them. Judgment will not so much be by what you have done in this life, but rather judgment will be accorded by what you have been called to do in this life and how well you accomplished that thing specifically!

> *And of the children of Issachar, which were men that had understanding of the times, to know what Israel ought to do; the heads of them were two hundred; and all their brethren were at their command.*
> 1 CHRONICLES 12:32

And yet there is still another warning for the believing Christian! How important it is for the Christian burden bearer to flow in the grace of Jesus Christ, least you become overburdened or offended.

> *Rejoice greatly, O daughter of Zion; shout, O daughter of Jerusalem: behold, your King comes to you: He is just, and having salvation; lowly, and riding upon an ass, and upon a colt the foal of an ass.*
> ZECHARIAH 9:9

To step out from the grace of God or attempt to enter some one else's call or situation without their grace is dangerous (Galatians 6:1 – 5). Stay in the grace that the Spirit has given to you – it is safe and it is good.

Is the nature of the lowly donkey operating within your life? Is the character of Jesus being carried along by your life and lifestyle?

Selah! – Stop and think on that.

The Sons of Thunder!

What is the fascination – this love/hate relationship our culture holds for the motorcycle? Men and women spend the entirety of their free time riding or repairing them, not to mention the thousands of dollars it may cost to customize one of these bikes! Often more expensive than a car and affording less safety and protection, they can be noisy as well as difficult for other traffic to see. So, what is it exactly that captivates us with such "big boy toys?" The motorcycle and the lifestyle with which it is shrouded have an exciting air that both at once calls to the rebellious as well as to the weekend adventurer seeking personal enjoyment and pleasure!

Times are changing. What once may have been the rule may now be the exception, but once upon a time motorcycles were more often associated with rebels or with what might be called a "free spirit." Now, a "free spirit" might be defined as a person who refuses to be conformed to the norm. And it is exactly for this reason that out of all the ministries of the Church it is the prophetic ministry which refuses to conform to the norm! It is this cutting edge ministry, whether found resident within a single persona or corporately within a church fellowship that stands as the Lord's fire brand. This ministry is sent from the Lord's heart (Ephesians 4:11) to demonstrate His love as well as declare His now word to both His Church and the world! It takes such a vanguard ministry to cut through the trappings of religious and cultural life that so weigh down and veil the truth of the Kingdom of God.

There is a reason that the term "thunder" is associated with a Harley Davidson motorcycle! Once while participating in a pastor's conference in Poznan, Poland (we were meeting at a church facility in the heart of the city), I was surprised and interrupted in the middle of my allotted time teaching by the thunder of hundreds and hundreds of motorcycles! These bikers had gathered from all over Poland and beyond for a rally, and they literally thundered by our meeting for fifteen to twenty minutes! Because of the noise, I had to suspend my preaching and simply stare out the windows with all the other pastors at this impromptu parade. Surely, James and John, the sons of Zebedee, must have ridden Harleys, for they were the original Sons of Thunder (Mark 3:17)!

The vanguard's proclamation

It is the motorcycle that is typically used as the forerunner or the vanguard of a motorcade. The word vanguard is defined from a combination of the Middle English word "vant" or guard and the Old French word avant-garde which means a pushing or extending of the boundaries of the acceptable or status quo. These vanguards were the troops who marched in front of the advancing main body of the army, or they were the leading position of a movement, or more specifically those leading the movement.[3] Synonyms for the word vanguard include forerunner, spearhead, advanced guard, first line of battle, outpost, bridgehead, beachhead, pioneer, precursor, pathfinder, front line, prototype, scout, explorer, point, bushwhacker, trailblazer, and guide.[4] Today's terminology might also include, Special Opts, Army Rangers or Navy Seals!

To continue with our analogy of the motorcade, as the main convoy passes, the forerunner was probably never seen or noticed by the vast majority of the crowd. And should this vanguard be seen, it is generally only a brief encounter, a momentary glance. Little attention is paid to this seemingly innocuous solitary motorcycle cruising down the parade route long before the actual motorcade is expected. And is it any wonder that children especially notice these lone motorcycle cops? They are fascinated by such things. They have a certain sensitivity to spiritual things as well. Jesus said,

> *Verily I say unto you, "Except you be converted, and become as little children, you shall not enter into the Kingdom of Heaven. Whosoever therefore shall humble himself as this little child, the same is greatest in the Kingdom of Heaven. And whoso shall receive one such little child in My name receives Me."*
>
> MATTHEW 18:3 – 5

Jesus also said of little children,

> *For the Kingdom of Heaven belongs to such as these.*
>
> MATTHEW 19:14

So while the crowd may miss these forerunners, the watchful eye of a child quickly notices. The majority of the crowd is only looking for and awaiting the main event, the dignitary and his/her entourage of multiple cars, flags, and fanfare. Isn't it interesting to note that only a very few ever really see the dignitary they've come to see, because of the vast crowds and clamour during the events! They rarely see the main person! It is so similar within the Church of Jesus Christ that many only see the hoopla and miss altogether the glory of the LORD! It is sad too, that many within the crowd often only see the event, the crowds of people, the excitement, the emotional exhilaration while missing the Reason for the event!

We see the prophetic and intercessory ministries stretching out and touching the glory of God and then calling the people of God, as well as the people of the world, to give an account before the LORD of Glory! The attestation of the presence and power of the Lord is seen in signs and wonders, miracles and demonstrations of the Spirit. It is this ministry's brash faith and boldness of character that acts as the catalyst or becomes the lightning rod of the Spirit! It is within the prophetic ministry that the lightnings and thunderings of God are often seen!

The ministry of the vanguard

Let's look at some of the characteristics that will be more or less common to this ministry of the motorcycle – the prophetic/vanguard ministry!

First, this prophetic/vanguard ministry bears the "now" word of the Lord. It has heard from the Spirit and acts immediately to implement and carry out what it has heard. Often impetuous and sometimes premature because of immaturity or lack of experience, it is this willingness to be spontaneous as well as unconventional that catches the attention of both society and the religious, and thus the wonder as well as the anger and envy of the people.

> *Surely the Lord GOD will do nothing, but He reveals His secret unto His servants the prophets.*
>
> AMOS 3:7

Secondly, the prophetic/vanguard ministry is a hidden ministry. Like John the Baptist, as he was in the wilderness "declaring the way of the Lord," this ministry will also be found ever pointing to Jesus as well as avoiding the limelight that Christ might increase and they might decrease! These hidden ministries have one intent – while shrinking from notoriety themselves, they want to see Jesus lifted up before men, and the Father receive the glory due His name.

> *He must increase, and I must decrease.*
>
> JOHN 3:30

Next, the prophetic/vanguard ministry is also a fiercely evangelistic ministry

> *...for the testimony of Jesus is the spirit of prophecy.*
>
> REVELATION 19:10

As hearts are revealed by the "now" word of the Lord and people are confronted by their own heart's sinfulness, many will turn to Messiah!

> *But if all of you are prophesying, and unbelievers or people who don't understand these things come into your meeting, they will be convicted of sin, and they will be condemned by what you say. As they listen, their secret thoughts will be laid bare, and they will fall down on their knees and worship God, declaring, "God is really here among you."*
>
> 1 CORINTHIANS 14:24 – 25 NLT

Evangelism is enhanced because this prophetic anointing is focused upon the person of Jesus. As prophetic ministry arises and is released within the confines of the Church the believers are themselves stirred and caught up in the same spirit and passion for Jesus. Sadly, this prophetic passion is not seen as often as it should be within our local assemblies. This prophetic and evangelistic anointing fan into flame once again the first love for the Saviour and with it is kindled a new eagerness to personal testimony and evangelism.

For I am jealous over you with godly jealousy: for I have espoused you to one husband that I may present you as a chaste virgin to Christ.
                                        2 CORINTHIANS 11:2

Fourth, the prophetic/vanguard community, like biker gangs or clubs – have heard the Spirit's call to community! The Church has a very clear divine call to be a prophetic community in the midst of this present world system with all of its darkness and death. It is the prophetic/vanguard ministry that is the Spirit's salt and light ever urging on the Church and the world rebellious!

That you may be blameless and harmless, the sons of God, without rebuke, in the midst of a crooked and perverse nation, among whom you shine as lights in the world; holding forth the Word of life; that I may rejoice in the day of Christ, that I have not run in vain, neither laboured in vain.
                                        PHILIPPIANS 2:15 – 16

You are the salt of the earth; but if the salt has become tasteless, how will it be made salty again? It is good for nothing anymore, except to be thrown out and trampled under foot by men. You are the light of the world. A city set on a hill cannot be hidden. Nor do men light a lamp, and put it under the bushel, but on the lamp stand; and it gives light to all who are in the house. Let your light shine before men in such a way that they may see your good works, and glorify your Father who is in heaven.
                                        MATTHEW 5:13-16 NASB

Finally, the prophetic/vanguard ministry understands how to labour in the realm of prayer and intercession.

Epaphras, who is one of you, a servant of Christ, salutes you, always labouring fervently for you in prayers that you may stand perfect and

> *complete in all the will of God. For I bear him record, that he has a great zeal for you, and those that are in Laodicea and in Hierapolis.*
>
> COLOSSIANS 4:12 – 13

With most every motorcade motorcycles proceed, surround, and even carry up the rear of the primary vehicle – the VIP vehicle. But there are those vanguard motorcycles (those patrol and scout cycles) that are ever vigilant and out along the designated travel route long before the main entourage ever comes into view! Unnoticed but by an observant few, perhaps especially the children, they cruise on ahead, alert and watchful.

It is in this same spirit of prophetic intercession that the spiritual vanguard labours in prayer. It is with a watchful eye upon the Master, and a shield and sword drawn to protect and defend the Body of Christ (Hebrews 12:2). It is within this ministry, united with Jesus, the ever living Intercessor, where battles are won before they are fought and where battles are engaged until victory is manifest (Hebrews 7:25). The prophetic intercessor gains their position of abiding at the Spirit's bidding and continues on in the Spirit's own strength of courage and endurance until victory is complete and finalized!

> *Humble yourselves therefore under the mighty hand of God, that He may exalt you in due time: casting all your care upon Him; for He cares for you. Be sober, be vigilant; because your adversary the devil, as a roaring lion, walks about, seeking whom he may devour: whom resist steadfast in the faith, knowing that the same afflictions are accomplished in your brethren that are in the world. But the God of all grace, Who has called us unto His eternal glory by Christ Jesus, after you have suffered a while, will make you perfect, establish, strengthen, and settle you. To Him be glory and dominion for ever and ever. Amen.*
>
> 1 PETER 5:6—11

Keen vision

The prophetic intercessor holds a vision many within the Body of Christ do not. Their vision is super charged with eternal realities and their stamina is fueled by the ever sustaining hope of the Gospel's power and ultimate victory! They press on long after others have grown weary and given up.

For Zion's sake will I not hold my peace, and for Jerusalem's sake I will not rest, until the righteousness thereof go forth as brightness, and the salvation thereof as a lamp that burns. ... I have set watchmen upon your walls, O Jerusalem, which shall never hold their peace day nor night: you that make mention of the LORD, keep not silence. And give Him no rest, until He establishes, and until He makes Jerusalem a praise in the earth. The LORD has sworn by His right hand, and by the arm of His strength ...Go through, go through the gates; prepare the way of the people; cast up, cast up the highway; gather out the stones; lift up a standard for the people. Behold, the LORD has proclaimed unto the end of the world, say to the daughter of Zion, "Behold, your salvation comes; behold, His reward is with Him, and His work before Him. And they shall call them, the holy people, the redeemed of the LORD and you shall be called, Sought out, a city not forsaken."

ISAIAH 62

Special Ops

But of course, the vanguard's mission is never to attract attention to its own assignment, but to prepare the way for the main event or person, who is yet to come. It is often a hidden work or ministry. In today's warfare, we hear of the "Special Ops" – the Navy Seals, Army Rangers, or covert CIA deep inside enemy's territory or a country long before hostilities erupt. Their task is to act as scouts uncovering surveillance details that reveal the enemy's every move, mapping their strategic targets, and detailing the enemy's timetables. Such information is then used to direct vital air strikes or artillery strikes at critical enemy targets long before the main deployment of Marine or Army troops come on the scene. Often they will have engaged the enemy first hand before the air power or naval bombardments begin.

Today's spiritual vanguards, like the Special Ops detachments, are labouring in prayer, wrestling with princes and powers, denying themselves in watches and fastings, to the glorious end that the captive be set free, that the Gospel be preached to the down trodden and oppressed, that salvation may visit the Spirit's targeted people! The King of kings will soon return to the earth in His triumphant procession. He is now gathering a people from every tongue, tribe and nation in the final harvest of the earth and all of this will have been preceded by His Special Ops of the Bikers and the Donkeys!

Such sacrifice and targeted ministry will always proceed the Church's experiencing revival and renewal! At times it is possible for these "special opts" to never taste for themselves – except by their faith – the victory the larger portion of the body of Christ will enjoy!

Time to ride

We can see it now! The ministries of the motorcycle and the donkey are more than relevant for our culture today! They are necessary and they are vital. How critical it is for these prophetic and intercessory ministries, these vanguard and front line ministries to be released to their place and destiny – speaking the "now" word of the Lord into our cultures and religious communities, not to mention our own personal lives!

John the Baptist (if he were here today), would surely ride a Harley. But on the other hand, his spirit would have been just as comfortable upon the humble donkey – as long as Jesus would be seen! Yes, John came it that spirit of Elijah!

> *Jesus began to say unto the multitudes concerning John, "...But what did you go out to see? A prophet? Yea, that's right, and more than a prophet. For this is he, of whom it is written, 'Behold, I send My messenger before Your face, and he shall prepare Your way before You. Verily I say unto you, among them that are born of women there has not risen a greater than John the Baptist: notwithstanding he that is least in the Kingdom of Heaven is greater than he. ...For all the prophets and the law prophesied until John. And if you will receive it, this is Elias, which was for to come. He that has ears to hear, let him hear.'"*
>
> MATTHEW 11:7 – 15

And that same call has gone out and it is resounding in the earth today—as the spirit of Elijah was upon John as he prepared the way of the Lord for Christ's first advent, so that same spirit of Elijah will be seen and felt in the nations of the earth before Messiah's Second Coming!

> *Behold, I will send you Elijah the prophet before the coming of the great and dreadful day of the LORD.*
>
> MALACHI 4:5

Today, Messiah has not only one prophet operating in the spirit of Elijah as He did when His cousin John preached in the wilderness, but these Special Ops are in every country – moving among every people, working signs and wonders, and proclaiming the soon coming of the King and His Kingdom!

Behold, I will send My messenger, and he shall prepare the way before Me...

MALACHI 3:1

The Last Day's Church imitating the bikers and the donkeys!

For those who can see it, the spirit of Elijah is upon the Church.

Behold, I will send you Elijah the prophet before the coming of the great and dreadful day of the LORD.

MALACHI 4:5

And the Church as a whole is called to bring Jesus into the arena of this present generation. It is not enough to leave the prophetic/vanguard ministries just to the Bikers and Donkeys, the Church as a whole must step into this role of Elijah and prepare the way of the Lord into our families, neighborhoods and cities. The sheep must be bold in their personal witness for Jesus Christ. The sheep must never be ashamed of the Gospel for it is the power of God unto salvation. (Romans 1:16). This present generation may indeed be the final generation before the return of the Lord Jesus Christ! And though we cannot say with a certainty this is the fact, we do know the time for Jesus' return surely is drawing ever nearer, ever closer! Yet for our generation, this is the last generation – this present generation will never have another opportunity to respond to the redemption found alone in Jesus Christ. It is a now or never proposition for millions!

It is appointed for man to die once and after that to face the judgment!

HEBREWS 9:27

Your generation is awaiting the message of the Lord Jesus Christ, and they are waiting to hear it through you!

Called to be salt and light we must know what is right and what is wrong, what is good and what is moral, what is evil and what is righteous?

Woe unto them that call evil good, and good evil; that put darkness for light, and light for darkness; that put bitter for sweet, and sweet for bitter!

ISAIAH 5:20

Called to be salt and light, we are allowing Jesus to remind others of His goodness through our lives. We are called to live holy – that is, we are called to live wholly unto the Lord, reflecting His righteousness so others can see Him through our daily living. And we are called to bear personal testimony for Jesus. We are to allow our words and lifestyle to constantly remind others of His personal invitation extended to them.

And the Spirit and the bride say, 'Come.' And let him that hears say, 'Come.' And let him that is athirst come. And whosoever will, let him take the water of life freely.

REVELATION 22:17

Called to bear witness to and for Jesus, our testimony of Jesus' Lordship brings life and light to our families, cities and governments. Each individual believer's calling in life and ministry is to live in such a way that those outside of Christ will be brought into a living awareness of Him as they enter into the arena of our lives.

These that have turned the world upside down are come here also.

ACTS 17:6

Called to train our senses to obey the Word of God rather than the whims of our old nature, we are to be consistently maturing and growing up in Christ. Such a witness in overcoming sin acts as a personal example showing forth a living God who is active and enabling within the believer's life.

For every one that uses milk is unskillful in the Word of righteousness: for he is a babe. But strong meat belongs to them that are of full age, even those who by reason of use have their senses exercised to discern both good and evil.

HEBREWS 5:13 – 14

Called to be a community of the Redeemed, we are Jesus' hands extended to others in need. We are called to be Jesus' mouthpiece of grace and forgiveness. We are called to be Jesus' wings of shelter to the hurting and broken. We are called to be a safe place where Jesus can bring healing to the hurting. We are called to be examples of Jesus' love to one another enabling the world to see the Living Christ in our midst. Such living offers a united front to the world that they might believe upon Jesus! (John 17:21; Ephesians 4:13—16).

Let us hold fast the profession of our faith without wavering for He is faithful that promised, and let us consider one another to provoke unto love and to good works not forsaking the assembling of ourselves together, as the manner of some is; but exhorting one another: and so much the more, as you see the day approaching.
HEBREWS 10:23 – 25

When community is broken, when vision is clouded, when purpose is thwarted, that is when Satan is exalted and his kingdom extended. But when faith's community is strong, when Heaven's vision is clear, when the Father's purpose is moving forward, that that is when Jesus will always be exalted and His Kingdom advanced...always!

So we can see that the forerunner, burden bearing ministry is prophetic by calling and definition, hidden by design and purpose and lowly by nature and character.

And therefore as individuals, each of us is called to prophetically prepare the way of the Lord into the lives and culture of those around us, living in such a manner as to draw attention to Jesus and not to ourselves and to demonstrate the character and nature of Jesus in all our dealings with men and society.

How can I tell if I'm a donkey, a biker or just a sheep?

Actually it can be rather difficult to tell whether you're a biker or a donkey or a sheep. But the bottom line for the believer is that he is called to look like Jesus, to follow Jesus, and to measure his/her own life by Jesus, not by the function or position of their ministry. We are first and foremost children of the Most High. Ministry that changes people and blesses people always flows out of our relationship with Christ.

In conclusion, it must be said lest we miss a very key point, that the prophetic/intercessory ministry never really tries to be prophetic. It is never really looking to be avant-garde. While they have general tendencies and natural inclinations simply because that is how God's giftings work within their lives, the prophetic/intercessor is never really looking for the "new" thing. Rather, this ministry, more often than not, serendipitously discovers that the Lord is leading or has led them into a new intercession or prophetic act – and all they have done to have arrived at this place is to simply have obeyed His leading. It is upon this discovery that they begin to apply their faith as well as their faithfulness to obtain the new place of abiding and thus are enabled to allow the Spirit to live, pray and act through them thus birthing His purposes and Kingdom in the earth.

...for as soon as Zion travailed, she brought forth her children.

ISAIAH 66:8c

As the intercession continues, as it deepens, the prophetic intercessor will be challenged with a whole new set of emotional and spiritual hurdles that must be fully acted out and embraced if the place of abiding is to be gained and thus the promised victory is to be obtained!

If you abide in Me, and My words abide in you, you shall ask what you will, and it shall be done unto you.

JOHN 15:7

No wonder there are trials that tempt us to quit and pressures that assail those called to this ministry to give up, to compromise or to stop altogether. To prevent or to impede this ministry would be to stop Christ. And since this ministry must precede the Christ's own coming our own success and victory is inevitable as is the inevitability of Jesus' return!

What shall we then say to these things? If God be for us, who can be against us?

ROMANS 8:31

Alleluia!

Cast not away therefore your confidence, which has great recompense of reward. For you have need of patience, that, after you have done the will of God, you might receive the promise. For yet a little while, and He that shall come will come, and will not tarry. Now the just shall live by faith; but if any man draws back, My soul shall have no pleasure in him. But we are not of them who draw back unto perdition, but of them that believe to the saving of the soul. Now faith is the substance of things hoped for, the evidence of things not seen.

HEBREWS 10:35 – 11:1

Never give up. Stay prayed up. Stay fasted up. Stay full and overflowing with the Word. Obey the Spirit quickly and completely. Watch and stay alert. Remain sensitive to the Lord's leading. Keep your gaze set upon Jesus. Let God be God.

Let us then assume the lowly and humble position of the donkey and "ride for Jesus!"

"Maranatha. Jesus come quickly!"

The Essence— the salvation of our God is an awesome thing and yet often believers miss out on those things that pertain to their peace and wholeness precisely because they have missed the visitation of God for their lives. In order for us to not miss the coming visitation of God we need to be prepared.

five

THE VISITATION OF GOD

THE VISITATION OF THE LORD IS an awesome thing! In the Greek the word visitation literally means an inspection. It also carries with it the meaning of superintendence (like the office of a bishop or overseer). In the Hebrew it refers to an official accounting, custody, or that which has been laid up. As the visitation of the Lord begins to move across a people or a nation, it is the Lord coming to inspect first His people and then those that remain.

> *...and the Lord, whom you seek, shall suddenly come to His temple, even the Messenger of the covenant, whom ye delight in; behold, He shall come, says the LORD of hosts. But who may abide the day of His coming? And who shall stand when He appears? For His is like a refiner's fire, and like fullers' soap. And He shall sit like a refiner and purifier of silver; and He shall purify the sons of Levi, and purge them like gold and silver, that they may offer unto the LORD an offering in righteousness.*
>
> MALACHI 3:1-3

And Simon Peter writes,

> *For the time is come that judgment must begin at the house of God; and if it first begins with us, what shall the end be of them that obey not the Gospel of God?*
>
> 1 PETER 4:17

While the visitation of God brings with it tremendous blessing, it can produce great fear as well within those whose hearts are not right before the Lord. It can also be seen that during these times of the Lord's visitation, tremendous miracles, signs, and wonders are released upon the people.

> *And by the hands of the apostles were many signs and wonders wrought among the people (and they were all with one accord in Solomon's porch).*
>
> ACTS 5:12

And yet, because it is a time of examination, a time when the Bishop of men's souls comes to make an inspection, we are required to give an accounting of our lives.

> *What is man, that You should magnify him and that You should set your heart upon him? And that You should visit him every morning, and try him every moment?*
>
> JOB 7:17 – 18

In the visitation of God experienced in Acts chapter 5, great signs and wonders were being done in the Name of Jesus. One couple, Ananias and his wife Sapphira, attempting to lie to the Holy Spirit and were found out by Peter. (Acts 5:1-17).

It is for this reason, the holiness and gracious character of the Lord, that many believers will never experience the full glory of His visitation. It is in His great mercy that He withholds from us this manifest glory, power, and presence. While we, the Church, have been purchased by the precious blood of Jesus and have had the righteousness of the Lord imparted to us, the Lord still demands that we walk in holiness.

> *But just as He who called you is holy, so be holy in all you do; for it is written: "Be holy, because I am holy."*
>
> 1 PETER 1:15-16

The same glory that heals is the same glory that judges. Ananias and Sapphira desired the blessing of God, but instead, discovered His judgment. If the same glory and power of the Lord were to enter our churches today, how many would be carried out?

This is one of the main reasons we have seen so many ministries and their leaders fall in disgrace. The Lord is preparing us for a visitation of His Spirit and in His mercy He is preparing us for a glorious season of harvest unparalleled in history. He would rather bless than judge.

God is on the move. The world is experiencing a move of God like no other ever seen upon the face of the earth. Now is the time of God's visitation. What some countries and peoples are now experiencing is unprecedented. This move of the Holy Spirit will cover the face of the earth sweeping millions into the Kingdom of God! We dare not miss this opportunity! This is the time for salvation! This is the time for deliverance! This is the time for healing! This is the time to call our friends, family and yes, even our enemies to the Savior. This is the time to worship freely and unashamedly! This is the time to cast yourself totally upon the Lord's goodness and mercy. This is the time to press into all the provision and abundance of the Father's storehouse. This is the time to say, "yes", to the Lordship of Jesus! This is the time to submit wholly to His will for our lives.

As Jesus beheld Jerusalem, He wept. He wept because His people did not understand and could not see that the day of the visitation of God was upon them and among them. Those things that "belonged to their peace", were in fact within their reach as He was there standing in their midst. And yet, they...

"knew not the time of their visitation."

LUKE 19:41-44

It is time for us, as the Church, begin to pray so that we might know the time of the Lord's visitation. It is time for us to press into all that the Lord is offering in this moment. It is time that we begin as never before to encourage one another to be awake, and not to sleep. We must stand ready to respond to all that the Lord would require of us. The Lord's heart cries out for us to not miss that which pertains to our peace and prosperity.

There was an old song, whose lyrics said, "Que sera, sera. Whatever will be, will be." This has been the attitude of many believers. "Whatever will happen will happen. God will take care of it." They even quote the Scriptures to reinforce their beliefs. And while our steps are indeed ordered of the Lord and our times are within His hands; our response is critical and our choices are important to our end. We are never promised a second chance, therefore choose wisely.

While God is moving, we must begin to respond to His leading and promptings. Whether it is concerning our personal walk with Jesus, our family life, our witness at work, our personal finances or hidden sin within our lives, now is the time for us to lay hold of Christ's presence, His peace and His forgiveness! He is ever present to release into our lives all that we have need of if only we will come ready to be changed. The visitation of the Lord is the time of His inspection! It is a time of His coming to make an official accounting to see what we have laid up in our personal accounts. In light of this, now is the time to press into the Kingdom!

As the pace increases toward the return of the Lord, it behooves us to establish ourselves as faithful servants, to become a people that understand the times that we might know what to do, and that we might be found abiding in the love of God, serving the brethren and zealous for good works (Titus 2.14; John 15.10; Matthew 25.21; Hebrews 10.24-25).

It is during the visitation of the Lord that hearts are revealed, judgment is executed and blessing comes. It is the visitation of the Lord that will preserve the righteous,

Thou hast granted me life and favor, and Thy visitation hath preserved my spirit.

JOB 10:12

It is the visitation of the Lord that will cause men's hearts to fail,

And what will ye do in the day of visitation, and in the desolation which shall come from far? To whom will ye flee for help? And where will ye leave your glory?

ISAIAH 10:3

It is the visitation of the Lord that will cause the ruin of the unjust and the exaltation of the righteous.

Were they ashamed when they had committed abomination? Nay, they were not at all ashamed, neither could they blush: therefore shall they fall among them that fall: in the time of their visitation they shall be cast down, saith the LORD.

EREMIAH 8:12

Having your conversation honest among the Gentiles: that, whereas they speak against you as evildoers, they may by your good works, which they shall behold, glorify God in the day of visitation.

1 PETER 2:12

The Church in America has been longing for and in desperate need of a major visitation of God, and there are wonderful evidences that it is gathering momentum of the Spirit rising in the land. However, we must recognize the time and prepare ourselves. If we are unprepared for this visitation of the Lord we will bring embarrassment and shame upon ourselves. But, if we recognize the signs of the times and are prepared to act with the Holy Spirit when this visitation manifests we will reap wonderful reward.

And shall lay thee even with the ground, and thy children within thee; and they shall not leave in thee one stone upon another; because thou knew not the time of thy visitation.

LUKE 19:44

Our prayer

Father, I am hungry for the things of Your Spirit and of Your Kingdom. I've grown weary with the sin and the spiritual laziness that I see and find within my own life. Grace me Lord to hunger and thirst after Your righteousness. May I not be satisfied until I am full and overflowing with Your life, Your holiness and Your power! Lord, I join my faith with thousands of other sincere believers who will not be satisfied with the spiritual status quo. We need another Great Awakening throughout the land. In Jesus' name, amen!

The Essence – As the winds of the Spirit begin to blow and God begins to effect change within His Church, we must be careful that past experiences, past traditions, past attitudes and present expectations do not hinder our ability to see and move in the next wave of God's Spirit.

six

AND THE WINDS BLEW

And the rain descended, and the floods came, and the winds blew, and beat upon that house; and it fell not: for it was founded upon a rock.
MATTHEW 7:25

THE LORD HAS ALWAYS had a current word for His people. He is no different today. He is a God Who speaks. He has a fresh, life-giving word for His people. Preparation has been made for a new and fresh release in the realm of the Spirit. However, there are also many other voices and "words" being spoken in today's world. None of us is isolated from these influences. It becomes vital then, that we learn to sift through that which is birthed by God's Spirit, that which issues forth from the heart of man, and that which is spewing forth from the demonic. Thank God, we have not been left to our own devices and ingenuity, but that we have God's Word and the Author of that Word to lead us into all truth!

The coming days will be critical in the life of the Church. The coming days will be critical concerning the nations. The destiny of millions of people is being decided. Nations and peoples are aligning themselves either with the purposes of God in the earth or they are careening into the future unaware of their sealed fate. There is growing evidence of a major visitation of God that is, even at this hour, sweeping the earth. It is a move unlike anything in history. It has various earmarks that may remind us of past renewals and awakenings, but there is something different, far greater, something far and away more wondrous.

The Lord has promised to reveal Himself in ever greater measures in the earth.

Of the increase of His government and peace there shall be no end, upon the throne of David, and upon His Kingdom, to order it and to establish

*it with judgment and with justice from henceforth even for ever. The zeal
of the LORD of hosts will perform this.*

ISAIAH 9:7

*'For thus says the LORD of Hosts; yet once, it is a little while, and I will
shake the heavens, and the earth, and the sea, and the dry land; and I
will shake all nations, and the desire of all nations shall come; and I will
fill this house with glory', says the LORD of Hosts. 'The silver is mine,
and the gold is mine, says the LORD of Hosts. The glory of this latter
house shall be greater than of the former', says the LORD of hosts: 'and
in this place will I give peace, says the LORD of hosts.'*

HAGGAI 2:6-9

The effect of this move of God's Spirit will not confined to small geographical areas or even to certain types of churches. Its ecclesiastical boundaries are unlimited. It appears to be the beginning of the final restoration of all things.

*Whom (Jesus) the heaven must receive until the times of restitution of all
things, which God hath spoken by the mouth of all His holy prophets
since the world began.*

ACTS 3:21

Its scope is global. Its magnitude is awesome. Its power is unrivaled.

*For the earth shall be filled with the knowledge of the glory of the LORD,
as the waters cover the sea.*

HABAKKUK 2:14

How sad that many are not even aware of this visitation! How grievous that many within the Church are not expecting it! How disturbing it is that many who have prayed and cried out for this revival are now angry and disillusioned at its coming! Did not Messiah's first advent scandalize most of the religious leaders of the day? They had become old wine skins (Mark 2:22). Were they not studied men? "Surely, they thought, "God would reveal Himself to us first! "Wouldn't He remain within the framework of our current beliefs and confessions?" But, He did not! How often the "framework" upon which we have built our lives and traditions, claiming them to be God's Holy Word, are merely boundaries of our own making—boundaries that in actuality confine and limit the Holy One of Israel.

Making the Word of God of none effect through your tradition...

MARK 7:13

Yea, they turned back and tempted God and limited the Holy One of Israel.

PSALM 78:41

It is the fallen nature of man that strives to force a limitless God into our limited thinking and biased definitions of God or of revival. Have we become so knowledgeable concerning the blessed Godhead that we actually believe that we know all of His thoughts and ways. Must He, as the heaven and earth's only true Sovereign, seek our permission to vary from our so very skillfully-crafted and thought-out plans and programs?

And when He was come near, He beheld the city, and wept over it, Saying, 'If you had known, even thou, at least in this your day, the things which belong unto your peace! But now they are hid from you. For the days shall come upon you, that your enemies shall cast a trench about you, and compass you round, and keep you in on every side, and shall lay you even with the ground, and your children within you; and they shall not leave in you one stone upon another; because you knew not the time of your visitation.'

LUKE 19:41-44

Often those who have been wonderfully used of God in the past become envious and jealous of those who have had a fresh touch of the Spirit. When our relationship with the Lord is allowed to grow stale, those who are having fresh encounters with Jesus are often seen or perceived as intimidating. Our definition of "true spirituality" is often determined by the degree of our own comfort and ease with our religious habits and dogma. Those believers, who are experiencing a new freshness in their Christian walk because of their new found intimacy with Jesus, reveal our own true stale spiritual condition. Our bankrupt spirituality becomes openly apparent by the sharp contrast of those who have learned the secret of drawing fresh provision from the accounts of Heaven. Why then are we so surprised by our soulish reactions to those receiving from the goodness of God? It is not enough for us to say we once had an encounter with God. We must draw fresh life from Him day by day. Sadly, many whose Christian walk has grown cold often view anything other than that which reflects their own experience as something foreign, something alien, or even something to be feared. Having had ourselves an authentic experience with the Lord, we are too often then biased by that same experience and may refuse to acknowledge as genuine anyone else's experience if it doesn't line up with our own. Our experiences and methods are not the measuring rod of spiritual experience – God's Word is that standard.

A rather humorous but profoundly poignant example reveals our hearts all too well. In the early nineteen seventies during the height of the Charismatic Renewal there were many books chronicling what God was doing in His church. One book told the story of how an older immigrant woman had had an incredible encounter with the Holy Spirit—while she was cleaning her oven! From that time on when she was praying for her friends, she would open the oven door and have them put their heads in the oven before she would pray for them! As ridiculous as this may seem, many were touched by the power of God in this lady's kitchen with their heads in her oven! First, it is amazing what people will do to receive something from God when they are spiritually hungry enough. And secondly, it is amazing how we believe others must receive from Him in the same way that we have received. We often think that the way we have experienced His life changing power is the only way God can do it. "After all, look at our denomination's founding fathers, past revivals, or this dear immigrant saint!" Today we would start a First Church of the Oven Door." We too often look to an experience rather than to the Lord, Who will tailor-make each experience for the specific individual all within the confines of His Word. In the cases of larger groups and denominations we often justify our current habits and customs with experiences that happened decades or even centuries ago. "Look what God did with them, and consequently, we must be the legitimate heirs!"

Then there is the story of a newlywed couple that will clarify the situation beautifully. As they were preparing an evening meal together, the man asked his bride why she was cutting up the pot roast when their pan was more than adequate to contain it. Her response was, "Well, my mother always did it that way." Now made curious by her husband's simply question, she decided to call her mother to learn her secrets of pot roast preparation. After a few minutes on the phone they discovered Mom, herself, didn't know why she prepared a pot roast the way she did. All she could say is "Well, that's the way Grandma always did it." Next our young bride calls Grandma to get to the bottom of this mystery. Grandma laughed and said, "I never owned a pot big enough to hold an entire roast, so I had to cut the roast in half and put it in two different pots!" I hope you're smiling, because we likewise continue to maintain and even force traditions upon people long after they have worn out their usefulness or long after we have forgotten why we even do what we do!

It is an issue of our world-view. Most often we humans have this outlook – we believe that our own world-view is the only correct and "untarnished" perspective. The real truth about our hearts when revealed can be both unfortunate and frightening—for you see, (we think to ourselves) all other Christian viewpoints have now become suspect. And so, we then force all subsequent generations who would be "in the faith" to ascribe to our certain mold and mindset. They are forced to defend our positions, attitudes, and actions because we "know" that ours is the only "true faith" – the only "true and orthodox faith." We cut up the pot roast whether or not it is needed. The consequence of these false judgments is that often we end up developing a "form of religion" that has denied the real life transforming power of the Gospel.

'Now faith is!"

HEBREWS 11:1

Genuine faith produces a living, vital relationship with the Master. Unless our faith produces a life-changing encounter with the risen Christ, we will end up propagating a lifeless form of religion, or at best, a godly people struggling to live up to a standard without any power to victoriously do so. These efforts often produce, not genuine spiritual offspring, but illegitimate offspring. These believers ultimately have no sense of spiritual security but rather must prop up a lifeless system of men's works and religious trappings. It is our responsibility as leaders within the Church to call for each generation to have its own fresh encounter with the Savior—an encounter with the risen Jesus, not an encounter with our programs, our doctrines, or our personalities. Often when an honest person begins to genuinely seek the Lord's heart and ways, we ostracize and pressure him to such a degree that, like Nicodemus, he must seek Jesus out in the dark of night, rather than find encouragement in his community of faith (John 3:1 – 2).

We need a personal, face-to-face encounter with the Living God! Each generation must see or sense its own heart-felt need for a personal encounter and experience with its Creator.

I have heard of You by the hearing of the ear: but now mine eye sees You.

JOB 42:5

No experience outside of an encounter with the living God will suffice. It is to Jesus alone we must turn.

There was a man of the Pharisees, named Nicodemus, a ruler of the Jews: the same came to Jesus by night, and said unto Him, 'Rabbi, we know that You are a teacher come from God: for no man can do these miracles that You do, except God be with him.' Jesus answered and said unto him, "Verily, verily, I say unto you, 'Except a man be born again, he cannot see the Kingdom of God.'" Nicodemus said unto him, 'How can a man be born when he is old? Can he enter the second time into his mother's womb, and be born?' Jesus answered, 'Verily, verily, I say unto you, except a man be born of water and of the Spirit, he cannot enter into the Kingdom of God. That which is born of the flesh is flesh: and that which is born of the Spirit is spirit. Marvel not that I said unto thee, you must be born again.'

JOHN 3:1-7

Regrettably we begin to attack the very things we have cried out to God to do for us. Recently, in a rather dramatic instance, we received a report from a brother on the foreign field concerning a number of people who had been raised from the dead. The testimony came from qualified men; men who have earned the right to be heard as credible witnesses. Upon sharing this with some godly men, one of their responses was this, "We must be careful; the devil does those kinds of things too." Say what? Incredible! Attributing the Holy Spirit's work to the devil because of the fear of something that is misunderstood or because it is from a doctrinal framework that will not permit the work of God's Spirit in ways that are outside our own person experience or denominational position is an all too familiar position church leaders take! We are to,

Prove all things; hold fast that which is good.

1 THESSALONIANS 5:21

But the proof is this—the devil is not in the resurrection business! His business is stealing, killing, and destroying (John 10:10). How insecure we must be! How pressured by a culture that demands performance and conformity! How easily intimidated by another's success! Are we not to call upon the Lord to establish His Kingdom? Is it not His glory that we seek? Should not our place be to stand in His presence and minister at His pleasure? Should we not rejoice with the other members of the Body of Christ when they rejoice and weep with them when they are grieved? Have we not yet grown weary with the shallowness of our own experience and walk with Jesus? Do we not long for a greater expression of His character and power within our lives? If we live after the flesh we will not only reap after the flesh, but will one day find ourselves treating with hatred and contempt, those who are walking in the Spirit and pleasing God!

> *But as then he that was born after the flesh persecuted him that was born after the Spirit, even so it is now.*
>
> GALATIANS 4:29

It is fundamental that we understand that the Lord has declared His Word to be unchanging and forever settled,

> *For ever, O LORD, Your Word is settled in heaven.*
>
> PSALM 119:89

We also need to realize that His Word is capable of speaking to us today in fresh and powerful ways that are relevant to our cultural and individual needs. The Word of God is the true manna sent from Heaven, and so, we need to have the revelation that it is truly living and powerful.

> *For the Word of God is quick, and powerful, and sharper than any two-edged sword, piercing even to the dividing asunder of soul and spirit, and of the joints and marrow, and is a discerner of the thoughts and intents of the heart.*
>
> HEBREWS 4:12

As the Spirit of God calls us to deeper levels of intercession and ministry, it is important that we yield to His Word in equal or greater proportion. As we are beginning to experience spiritual manifestations that are outside the context of what we would call "normal," it is critical that we continue to establish this generation in the Word of God. Our thinking needs to be based upon the Word of God not on past experience or past revivals. It is critical for us to be sure that we are equipping our people to "think from the Word of God, not merely to the Word of God." It is mandatory for the Bride of Christ to build equity in the Word of God—to hide the Bridegroom's Word within her heart. She must honor that Word and live it out obediently and joyously. She must embrace even that which is not comfortable. It is important that stubbornness and unbelief be rooted out. It is vitally important that we yield our haughtiness and pride and begin to walk in a newness of humility and brokenness at the Master's feet. It is essential that we allow Jesus to reign in all our ways, thoughts, and yes, even our doctrines.

Past experiences and revivals may be sign posts for us that help us gauge our present position in the ongoing flow of the Kingdom, but they are not capable of dictating to us our current place in those things of God, but we must also cultivate a close and personal relationship with the Author of the Word – the Holy Spirit.

Equally important is that we allow the Holy Spirit to lead us as our Guide both through the Word and the times in which we find ourselves! He is the ever Present One knowing our specific circumstances and personalities. He has immediate access to the mind of the Father and the heart of the Saviour. He will keep us from taking a wrong turn – even when we are using the map – the Bible. He will fan into flame our passion to follow Jesus and offer us the discernment to press in to the things of God without fear of deception. His is the endurance and inner strength we need to face these Ending Days when our own strength and courage may fail us.

> *And he said, 'The LORD is my rock, and my fortress, and my deliverer; the God of my rock; in Him will I trust: He is my shield, and the horn of my salvation, my high tower, and my refuge, my Saviour; You save me from violence. I will call on the LORD, who is worthy to be praised: so shall I be saved from mine enemies. When the waves of death compassed me, the floods of ungodly men made me afraid; The sorrows of hell compassed me about; the snares of death prevented me; in my distress I called upon the LORD, and cried to my God: and He did hear my voice out of His temple, and my cry did enter into His ears... Then the earth shook and trembled; the foundations of heaven moved... The LORD lives; and blessed be my rock; and exalted be the God of the rock of my salvation.*
> 2 SAMUEL 22:2 – 8, 47

It is upon this rock of the Word of God, the Lord Jesus Himself, that we will find a safe and unshakable haven.

> *And the rain descended, and the floods came, and the winds blew, and beat upon that house; and it fell not: for it was founded upon a rock.*
> MATTHEW 7:25

The Spirit of the Lord is calling us into the deeper waters. Our faith will be challenged and at times our minds may be offended, yet the call goes out. "Launch out into the deep for a catch!" Will we, like Peter respond in faith to the Master's call? Or will we resist the direction and anointing of the Spirit, the Lord within the Church?

The Essence – It is easy enough to see the aftermath of a tsunami for it leaves in its wake a wide swath of destructive power. However, before this awesome force actually advances onto the coast there is a swift recession of normal waters before the massive tidal wave races ashore. Likewise, before a great revival or outpouring of the Spirit, many individuals may experience a receding of the tangible presence of the Lord and many churches may experience a rapid falling away of its people and/or resources before the advancement of the Kingdom comes in the form of a spiritual tsunami full of the glory of God.

seven

THE COMING TSUNAMIS OF REVIVAL
(FINDING SIGNS OF HOPE IN THE MIDST OF TROUBLE)

WHAT MAY SEEM LIKE THE SIGNS of failure and utter defeat, if seen through the eyes of the Spirit may actually be the evidences of a quickly approaching tidal wave of God's power and glory!

> *These trials are only to test your faith, to show that it is strong and pure. It is being tested as fire tests and purifies gold - and your faith is far more precious to God than mere gold. So if your faith remains strong after being tried by fiery trials, it will bring you much praise and glory and honor on the day when Jesus Christ is revealed to the whole world. You love Him even though you have never seen Him. Though you do not see Him, you trust Him; and even now you are happy with a glorious, inexpressible joy.*
>
> 1 PETER 1:7 – 8 NLT

Life, like the ocean's waves, ebbs and flows. However, these waves of life are often not as consistent or at least perceivably consistent as the tides of the seas. We have tide clocks and charts that predict with wonderful accuracy when we may expect the high and low tides. Because of the Creator's fine tuning of the worlds, men have invented instruments and means of forecasting these rhythms of the seas, even enabling us to predict with great precision the tides annual highs and lows – consistently to the minute.

Spiritual laws, like natural laws, are predictable. However, because we can not see into the hearts of men, at times, things appear cloudy.

Judgments and discernments are often biased by our experiences or by the emotional favoritism or prejudices we hold. None the less, there is a spiritual tide ebbing and flowing all around us. We see it in large scale throughout the book of Judges. These forty year cycles saw the blessing of God upon the people of Israel and their subsequent failure to walk righteously before God. Their disobedience produced a waning of the blessing of God and literally empowered their enemies to plunder their lives and land. Repentance and heartfelt prayer of the people would release, once again, the compassion of God in the form of regional and national judges who would bring deliverance from Israel's enemies along with the accompanying blessing of the Lord.

> *If you'll be willing and obedient, you shall eat the good of the land: but if you refuse and rebel, you shall be devoured with the sword: for the mouth of the LORD hath spoken it.*
> ISAIAH 1:19 – 20

We expect natural laws to work. We never question them. And as there are natural laws working in the earth (laws of gravity, aerodynamics, etc.) so there are various laws and principles of spiritual truth working all around us as well. These spiritual truths are not hidden but are so taken for granted that it becomes easy for us to overlook them or discount them. We never fully apply an active and vital faith (another spiritual law) to the circumstances we face. Sadly, we miss the power that God has made available to us by His Spirit to overcome the obstacles we face or the miracles we need.

As we face the last of the Last Days there are parts of the world enjoying unprecedented moves of the Spirit of God. Apostolic signs and wonders are once again flowing through the people of God to a sinful, lost, and needy world. These mighty signs and wonders are the Church's spiritual birthright. They should be welcomed. They should be expected. They should be encouraged. They should be cultivated. They should be active in every believer's life to one degree or another.

Whether major cultural shaping awakenings or more localized outpourings of the Spirit, we can make an observation from the rhythms and anomalies of the ocean. These principles are evident in the lives of individuals and within the framework of the local church. They are seen on regional levels as well as in national moves of the Spirit of God. There will always be, it seems, (this side of heaven), an ebb and flow to the things of God.

The tsunami example

The tsunami is the most dangerous and terrifying of waves. Its speed is amazing and its size is immense. Its destruction can be incomprehensible and its arrival surprising. Though modern science and technologies have helped in the early detection of tsunamis they still remain a formidable threat to heavily populated coastal areas. For the informed, a tsunami almost always generates it own early warning system, albeit extremely short in duration. As such, the tsunami holds a great spiritual lesson for us. We will learn that the coming tsunami has markers that give the watchful eye (and ear) a warning of what is about to transpire. As we discover these indicators we'll then be better equipped to apply these signs to the ebb and flow of the Holy Spirit's moving in the current spiritual climate.

In an article from the Georgia Institute of Technology the author stated that on July 17, 2006, a 65 foot "stealth" tsunami killed 600 in Java, Indonesia.[5] This same article reported that...

"...though categorized as magnitude 7.8, the earthquake could scarcely be felt by beachgoers that afternoon. A low tide and wind-driven waves disguised the signs of receding water, so when the tsunami struck, it caught even lifeguards by surprise. That contributed to the death toll of more than 600 persons in Java, Indonesia."

"The general assumption was that if you were near the coast where the earthquake took place, you would feel it and be able to run to higher ground," said Hermann Fritz, first author of a new Geophysical Research Letters paper about the July 17, 2006 tsunami. "This event caught people by surprise and showed that it's not always that simple."

..."Warning systems typically don't work very well for locations near earthquakes, where there are only tens of minutes between the earthquake and the tsunami's arrival," noted Fritz, a Georgia Institute of Technology assistant professor who led an inspection team to Java a week after the event. "It's pretty much a spontaneous self-evacuation. You normally feel the earthquake or see the ocean withdraw. If you hear the noise in the last tens of seconds before it hits, then it's just a matter of who makes it and who doesn't."

...For people in seismically-active areas like Indonesia, an earthquake usually provides the first warning of a tsunami. Whether caused by

an earthquake or an underwater landslide, the first visible sign of an oncoming tsunami is often a rapid withdrawal of the ocean that exposes the seafloor or coral reefs. When that appears, the first tsunami wave won't be far behind.

In the July 2006 Java tsunami, lifeguards did not notice the withdrawal because the water was receding anyway because of a normal low tide - and because of large wind-produced waves.

"The lifeguards did not recognize the precursors of the tsunami, either the shaking of the earth or the drawing down of the sea," said Fritz, who also interviewed survivors of the 2004 Indonesian tsunami. "The irony is that many of the lifeguards survived because they were in tall concrete structures sitting more than four meters above the ground, getting just their feet wet - a classic example of vertical evacuation in engineered structures.

...A tsunami normally produces more than one wave, and the waves can be 10 or 20 minutes apart. Often, the second or third wave is the largest, so many deaths occur when victims return to low-lying areas to look for relatives or assess damage after the first wave hits.

However, when they approach land, the waves slow as their height builds and energy dissipates. By the time they roll onto a beach, the waves may be moving at vehicle highway speed, but that quickly drops as they encounter structures and vegetation.

"If you start running from the beach when the tsunami strikes, chances are you are not going to make it," Fritz said. "But if you have a head-start, you have a much better chance - if you know where you're going."

Natural phenomenon – Spiritual application

To reiterate what is happening, we have learned that as a tsunami approaches a coastal area, the waters between the wave and the coast itself begin to recede or rush out to meet the gigantic wave as it is racing toward shore. It will begin to build in height and to slow down considerably, although it is still racing much too fast to out run it on foot. There will also be a new sound coming from off-shore as these quickly receding waters and then the swiftly moving incoming waters are racing over exposed coral and rocks. Once this chaotic sound is heard there may not be time to escape.

If we apply this natural phenomenon to the spiritual world all around us we discover that when we see the waters around us receding, rather than panic, we may with confidence hold a great expectation of God's soon arrival upon the scene! Yes, there is hope in the midst of what is an apparent failing or in spite of the disappointments being experienced – you must train yourself to look past what you are currently experiencing in the natural or with what you can see only with the natural eye! Frequently the troubles we're experiencing with people, the various spiritual attacks, or the disillusionments we must face all mask the Lord's under riding purpose of bringing revival and refreshing to our lives.

For our light affliction, which is but for a moment, works for us a far more exceeding and eternal weight of glory; while we look not at the things which are seen, but at the things which are not seen: for the things which are seen are temporal; but the things which are not seen are eternal.

2 CORINTHIANS 4:17 – 18

For we walk by faith, not by sight.

2 CORINTHIANS 5:7

This spiritual phenomenon of the pre-tsunami-like receding of waters has been experienced by many within the Church. From our own national history we may clearly see the accounts of the terrible spiritual and moral declines just prior to America's First and Second Great Awakenings! Not seeing the rising tide of God's blessing and glory over the horizon of our own personal troubles and the struggles of day to day living we can easily miss this tsunami of God which is about to wash over the Church. And sadly, there are those in the church, who like the receding waters before a natural tsunami, withdraw their presence from the assembly of believers. Whether by persecution or tribulation, whether by the fearful pulling back of full-out commitment to the things of God, or the easily offended personalities responding out of immaturity, many will miss the coming tsunami glory wave and like those victims of a devastating tsunami, end up with lives in spiritual shipwreck or spiritually bankrupt.

Holding faith, and a good conscience; which some having put away concerning faith have made shipwreck...

Mark D. Spencer

1 TIMOTHY 1:19

As a wave of revival begins, it too, may be rather "noisy." It may appear to the casual observer or the strict legalist that all is out of order and that things are in disarray. Such disorder can easily appear to the undiscerning that what is transpiring has not been initiated by the Holy Spirit, but rather, by another spirit. This sort of quick judgment without the wisdom of God will often dampen faith and "quench the Spirit." We must understand the workings of the Spirit if we are to enjoy the benefits of His unleashed presence. To insist on being a "control freak" may just bar your church fellowship from the liberty and life changing power of a God-sent revival. We must discern and know the ways of the Lord lest we become like the people of the world who are without a covenant and without hope. Many promising outpourings of the Spirit have been resisted and squelched by good intentioned and sincere people – they were sincerely mistaken.

Oh that My people had hearkened unto Me, and Israel had walked in My ways! I should soon have subdued their enemies, and turned My hand against their adversaries.

PSALM 81:13 – 14

Forty years long was I grieved with this generation, and said, "It is a people that do err in their heart, and they have not known My ways." Unto whom I swore in My wrath that they should not enter into My rest.

PSALM 95:10 – 11

To see and walk in the ways of the Lord is to ultimately walk in His blessing. To understand His ways is to be empowered to then flow with Him and to experience the good outcome of the life of obedience.

Now therefore hearken unto Me, O ye children: for blessed are they that keep My ways.

PROVERBS 8:32

There are it seems, few men or women who really understand or know the ways of God, and fewer who know them intimately. While the Lord has extended His invitation to all who are hungry and to all who are thirsty to come and receive what He would graciously offer, sadly, only a sparse few will ever lay claim to the full provision and abundant supply of the Spirit. Determine now, with the Holy Spirit's help, to be that one in a thousand who will dare believe what God has promised and seize all that God has offered!

> *But we are not of those who shrink back to destruction, but of those who have faith...*
>
> HEBREWS 10:39a,b NASB

There is rising up out of the peoples of the earth a generation who can and will accomplish all that the Lord wishes – a people who will respond quickly to the promptings of the Spirit and who will honour the Word of God. Such will see the glory of God in an unsurpassed measure and they will usher in the Lord at His soon coming! Knowing the various signs of His manifestation may at times be difficult to discern, but to the one who has walked with God consistently, the ever familiar sound of the Master's voice will ring true to their hearts and be born out in their experience.

> *My sheep hear My voice, and I know them, and they follow Me.*
>
> JOHN 10:27

This tsunami of the glory of God "will cover the earth as the waters cover the seas!" Miracles, signs, and wonders will flow in even greater measure than the days of the apostles – indeed apostolic days are once again approaching and they are laden with "greater works than these shall you do" (Habakkuk 2:14; John 14:12). That which the prophets foresaw will be manifest before our very eyes and through our very hands.

> *"The glory of this latter house shall be greater than of the former," says the LORD of hosts. "And in this place will I give peace," says the LORD of hosts.*
>
> HAGGAI 2:9

The key to victory in all of life's difficulties and throughout all of life's challenges is to know the God of Victory!

> *"...but the people that do know their God shall be strong, and do exploits."*
>
> DANIEL 11:32b

Mark D. Spencer

Let's lift up our heads and hearts with a certain expectancy of the soon manifestation of the glory of God leading to the glorious return of Jesus Christ. To this end we must run the second mile with the same intensity and determination we ran the first mile. To this end we must pray and fast with a renewed resolve that our faith is making a difference and that it is found pleasing to God. To this end we must not look at present difficult circumstances of life but press on into the things and realms of the Spirit where we will both hear and see the sound of rushing waters!

Blow ye the trumpet in Zion, and sound an alarm in My holy mountain: let all the inhabitants of the land tremble: for the day of the LORD cometh, for it is nigh at hand.

JOEL 2:1

Sound the shofar – there is a tsunami of the glory of God coming!

The Essence – These last of the Last Days will be punctuated with terrible and awesome deeds of righteousness! The earth and its people will experience once again the gloriousness and awesomeness of the Living God! This clarion call of the Spirit includes a cry for intercessors to believe with Him for the release of such Ending Days' awesome deeds in righteousness!

eight

AWESOME DEEDS IN RIGHTEOUSNESS

*By terrible things (awesome deeds) in righteousness You will answer us,
O God of our salvation; You who are the confidence of all the ends of the
earth, and of them that are afar off upon the sea.*

PSALM 65:5

IT IS TIME! TIME FOR the Church, as well as the nations of the
world to experience once again the awesome deeds of our God!

While miracles, signs, and wonders have never ceased within the
Church Age, as so many would tell us, there have been periods of time
where the manifested glory of God has subsided from the realms of men
much as the waters of coastal lands experience the rhythmic ebb and flow
of the tides. But, the tide of God's Shekinah glory is rapidly rising!

Rolling up His sleeves

*"Repent, then, and turn to God, so that your sins may be wiped out, that
times of refreshing may come from the Lord, and that He may send the
Christ, who has been appointed for you, even Jesus. He must remain in
heaven until the time comes for God to restore everything, as He promised
long ago through His holy prophets."*

ACTS 3:19-21 NIV

Heaven is awaiting with eager anticipation the restoration of all things!
The last one hundred to three hundred years has seen the restoration of
the apostolic minded ministries and churches in the earth that are wholly

dedicated, not to man's agendas or promotion, but rather to seeing Jesus exalted and declared among the nations and peoples of the world!

And now it's our Father's turn! He is preparing to bare His arm and demonstrate Himself to a watching world.

> *The LORD hath made bare His holy arm in the eyes of all the nations;*
> *and all the ends of the earth shall see the salvation of our God.*
>
> ISAIAH 52:10

Yes, Jesus is the Arm of the Lord that has already been bared in the earth. He is the pinnacle of all the wonders of God, but even now, it is as if the Lord of the Harvest is rolling up His sleeve in preparation to enter this final harvest – personally supervising these final moments of Ending Days labors before time is over!

> *For these are not drunken, as ye suppose, seeing it is but the third hour*
> *of the day. But this is that which was spoken by the prophet Joel; and*
> *it shall come to pass in the last days, says God, 'I will pour out of My*
> *Spirit upon all flesh: and your sons and your daughters shall prophesy,*
> *and your young men shall see visions, and your old men shall dream*
> *dreams: and on My servants and on My handmaidens I will pour out*
> *in those days of My Spirit; and they shall prophesy: and I will show*
> *wonders in heaven above, and signs in the earth beneath; blood, and fire,*
> *and vapour of smoke: The sun shall be turned into darkness, and the*
> *moon into blood, before that great and notable day of the Lord come: and*
> *it shall come to pass, that whosoever shall call on the name of the Lord*
> *shall be saved.' Ye men of Israel, hear these words; Jesus of Nazareth, a*
> *man approved of God among you by miracles and wonders and signs,*
> *which God did by Him in the midst of you, as ye yourselves also know.*
>
> ACTS 2:15-22

As these prophecies were true two thousand years ago, surely they are even more pertinent in these final closing moments of history! This is surely not the time for sleep – there is far too much to miss – and far too much work to be done!

> *Awake, O sleeper, rise up from the dead, and Christ will give you light.*
>
> EPHESIANS 5:14

Some of the evidences of the Lord bearing His mighty arm in the earth will be the signs, wonders and miracles He does through the believing people of God. Not only should we be expect signs, wonders and miracles, but our faith should be rising for the Lord to release, once again in the earth, His awesome deeds in righteousness!

Defining our terms

Miracle. The word "miracle" comes from the Greek word "dunamis" where we derive our English word for dynamite. It speaks of power, strength, and a mighty or wonderful work. The 1828 Webster Dictionary defines it "to wonder," literally then "a wonderful thing." Further, a miracle is "an event or effect contrary to the established constitution and course of things, or a deviation from the known laws of nature; a supernatural event. Miracles can only be worked by Almighty power, as when Christ healed the lepers... or calmed the tempest." We may conclude then that a miracle is the suspension of natural law by the higher law of the Spirit of Life in Christ Jesus!

The truth is, anyone who believes in Me will do the same works I have done, and even greater works, because I am going to be with the Father.
                                                                        JOHN 14:12 NLT

Wonder. The word "wonder" is defined by the 1828 Webster Dictionary as "the emotion which is excited by novelty, or the presentation to the sight or mind, of something new, unusual, strange, great, extraordinary, or not well understood; something that arrests the attention by its novelty, grandeur or inexplicableness..." We might say then that a wonder is something the Lord does to gain our notice, something that literally arrests our mind's attention!

...and they were filled with wonder and amazement at that which had happened unto him.
                                                                        ACTS 3:10

Or as the New Living Translation says, "they were absolutely astounded!"

Sign. A sign is a token; "something by which another thing is shown or represented; any visible thing, any motion, appearance or event which indicates the existence or approach of something else." It is an indication of a remarkable transaction, event or phenomenon. It is a visible transaction, event or appearance intended as proof or evidence of something else.

Mark D. Spencer

And I will show wonders in heaven above, and signs in the earth beneath; blood, and fire, and vapour of smoke: the sun shall be turned into darkness, and the moon into blood, before that great and notable day of the Lord come.

ACTS 2:19-20

Jesus demonstrated all three – miracles, signs and wonders.

Ye men of Israel, hear these words; Jesus of Nazareth, a man approved of God among you by miracles and wonders and signs, which God did by Him in the midst of you, as ye yourselves also know.

ACTS 2:22

Others have walked in these same amazing expressions of the Kingdom of God as well.
Stephen...

And Stephen, full of faith and power, did great wonders and miracles among the people.

ACTS 6:8

Paul...

And God wrought special miracles by the hands of Paul.

ACTS 19:11

The Twelve...

God also bearing them witness, both with signs and wonders, and with divers miracles, and gifts of the Holy Ghost, according to His own will?

HEBREWS 2:4

You and me...

Truly, truly, I say to you, he who believes in Me, the works that I do shall he do also; and greater works than these shall he do because I go to the Father.

JOHN 14:12 NASB

What then is an "awesome deed"?

An awesome deed may be classified as a miracle, but a miracle, a sign, or a wonder is not necessarily an awesome deed!

Awesome. The word awesome comes from the word 'awe', meaning to strike with fear and reverence; to influence by fear, terror or respect. It is a fear mingled with admiration or reverence; reverential fear. "Stand in awe, and sin not" (Psalm 4:4). It further means a dreadful or terrible act. Such definitions may at times confuse our theologies and fog our thinking. Therefore, the term "awesome deeds in righteousness" may be better clarified by example than by definition. The act of Creation, the death of Egypt's first born, the parting of the Red Sea and subsequent utter annihilation of Pharaoh's armies, Joshua's command to stop the sun in its course, or Isaiah's prayer for the sun to reverse its course – these are true "awesome deeds in righteousness!" And at the pinnacle of awesome deeds in righteousness is the resurrection triumph of our Lord, Jesus Christ – Alleluia!

Two aspects of awesome deeds

As the Word of God, the sword of the Spirit, is two-sided – one side as an offensive weapon to use against our spiritual enemies – and one side to use on our own soulishness – so awesome and terrible deeds in righteousness may manifest both sides of the blessing and the curse of God (Matthew 4:1-11; Hebrews 4:12; Deuteronomy 28). Aaron's Rod demonstrated this two-sidedness of an awesome deed – though only in type (Numbers 16 & 17). Clearly seen is the judgment by God as the rebels are immediately and finally judged. As well, we can clearly see the blessing and authority of God released upon the possessor of Aaron's Rod.[6] We must understand the two-fold nature of an awesome deed in righteousness lest we miss the opportunity the Spirit of God is affording us to proclaim the Good News and the Son's coming Kingdom!

Yet have I set My King upon My holy hill of Zion. I will declare the decree: the LORD hath said unto Me, 'You are My Son; this day have I begotten you. Ask of Me, and I shall give You the nations for Your inheritance, and the uttermost parts of the earth for Your possession. You shall break them with a rod of iron; You shall dash them in pieces like a potter's vessel.' Be wise now therefore, O kings be instructed, judges of the earth. Serve the LORD with fear, and rejoice with trembling. Kiss

the Son, lest He be angry, and you perish from the way, when His wrath
is kindled but a little. Blessed are all they that put their trust in Him.

PSALM 2:6-12

Past awesome deeds in righteousness revisited

The Exodus was a period of time where awesome deed after awesome
deed revealed both to the Israelite nation and to the Egyptian nation
just who Yahweh was! These awesome deeds in righteousness judged
idols and false gods through plagues that swept over the land at
Moses' command of faith or outstretched rod. These awesome deeds
in righteousness repaid four hundred and thirty years of back wages
owed the Jewish people by the Egyptian government. Though bound as
slaves under the worst of conditions, these now free men left the land of
their captivity with not one feeble among them! These awesome deeds
in righteousness fed and clothed, cooled and warmed, protected and
delivered, judged and buried millions of people in the midst of a desert
– for forty years!

Joshua, the captain of the armies of Israel, is in the midst of a
great battle. In this battle Joshua has seen the Lord rain down huge
hailstones on Israel's enemies. But even now, with the battle victory
surely theirs, Joshua must yet fight another foe – darkness. Joshua,
knowing the God he serves, stands and issues the command of faith,
and demands that the sun stand still in the heavens so that Israel
might have a complete and utter victory (Joshua 10)! And if that is
not enough we see in the book of Judges that the very stars fought on
Israel's behalf!

*They fought from heaven; the stars in their courses fought against
Sisera.*

JUDGES 5:20

And yet there are more awesome deeds in righteousness. Together,
Isaiah the prophet and Hezekiah the king, experience their own
awesome deed in righteousness. When Isaiah asks if Hezekiah would
like a sign from the Lord to confirm His promised healing of the king's
body, Isaiah offers to move the sun forward in the sky. Hezekiah
responds to the prophet by saying that such a miracle would be too
easy, for the sun will move that direction anyway. The challenge is
taken up and sun is again moved in its course. Only this time at Isaiah's

command of faith the sun, amazingly, moves backward through the sky! Our minds reel under such possibilities though our spirits cry out like a small child who squeals when their daddy has tossed them playfully up into the air, "More Daddy!" So, the Church in this hour is crying, "More Abba!"

Awesome deeds in righteousness and the Ending Days

Yes, "the word is on the street." Abba is about to demonstrate Himself before the whole of the earth and its people. The return of Jesus Christ is imminent. He is preparing to once and for all take up His throne in Jerusalem and rule the nations with a rod of iron.

> *And out of His mouth goes a sharp sword, that with it He should smite the nations and He shall rule them with a rod of iron and He treads the winepress of the fierceness and wrath of Almighty God. And He hath on His vesture and on His thigh a name written, KING OF KINGS, AND LORD OF LORDS.*
>
> REVELATION 19:15 – 16

The peoples of the world are experiencing and will soon see an increase in the very pre-return signs that trumpet the Lord's return.

> *And I will show wonders in heaven above, and signs in the earth beneath; blood, and fire, and vapour of smoke. The sun shall be turned into darkness, and the moon into blood, before that great and notable day of the Lord come.*
>
> ACTS 2:19 – 20

One only need read through the Book of Revelation to come to the conclusion that the awesome deeds of righteousness of the Exodus will pale in the face of the awesome deeds that await us in the waning moments of time! The two witnesses of Revelation will demonstrate such awesome deeds in righteousness to the world and its corrupt leaders, that when they are finally overcome by the anti-Christ, the world will rejoice because such judgments will have finally – or so they erroneously suppose – have ceased (Revelation 11).

Mark D. Spencer

How can we begin to believe for these awesome deeds?

"My Creed leads me to think that prayer is efficacious, and surely a day's asking God to overrule all events for good is not lost. Still there is a great feeling that when a man is praying he is doing nothing, and this feeling makes us give undue importance to work, sometimes even to the hurrying over or even to the neglect of prayer.

Do not we rest in our day too much on the arm of flesh? Cannot the same wonders be done now as of old? Do not the eyes of the Lord run to and fro throughout the whole earth still to show Himself strong on behalf of those who put their trust in Him? Oh that God would give me more practical faith in Him! Where is now the Lord God of Elijah? He is waiting for Elijah to call on Him."

JAMES GILMOUR OF MONGOLIA

Where are the Elijahs, the Moses', and the Pauls? Why is it necessary to believe for awesome deeds in righteousness? Won't God merely act when He is ready? Something for us to consider – why is it that people typically get saved or healed in churches that preach salvation and healing? Why doesn't the Lord sovereignly show up in a secularized church or in public government schools and just save everyone? Why doesn't He just visit hospitals and heal all the sick folks? It's not that He doesn't want those people saved or healed, but He has chosen to work through the medium of willing men and women whom He can send! Indeed James Gilmour of Mongolia, where are the Elijahs?

Daniel was such an Elijah, called of God to intercede and believe for the unfolding of end time events. We often miss that many of these revelations came because Daniel refused to simply say, "I saw in the writings of Jeremiah the prophet that our captivity in Babylon would only be seventy years so I guess the Lord will act any day now." Of course he didn't respond this way! Rather he began to fast and seek God to fulfill the promise of His Word (Daniel 9:2). And the call is the same for us today. The Spirit of God is looking for someone to enter the yoke with Him and begin to believe for these Ending Days' terrible and awesome deeds in righteousness!

This charge I commit unto you, son Timothy, according to the prophecies which went before on you, that by them you might wage a good warfare.

Are you the Elijah the Spirit of God is looking for to join with Him in this great work? Maybe you're a Daniel or a Paul? Where is the Deborah or the Mary who is prepared to yield completely to the will of God?

"Be it done unto me according to Your Word."

LUKE 1:38

It is time for us to personally respond to the call of the Spirit that is going out in this hour, and for this, our generation.

Personally, what will an awesome deed in righteousness look like?

As with all spiritual truths, no matter how out of reach they may seem to the average or ordinary believer like us, the Lord will always, always enable us and encourage us to expect His mighty workings within our own lives. Yes, we are called to believe for the greater manifestations of His glory in the earth, but as our Father, He invites us to believe Him for miracles, signs, wonders and even awesome deeds in righteousness right outside in own back yard, so to speak! As we see the Consummation of the Ages so quickly approaching we need to latch hold with our faith. And if nothing else, the residual blessing of faith and glory will more than meet any need you may have (2 Kings 13:21; Acts 19:12). As we believe for the larger sphere of awesome deeds, we can expect their manifestation to meet whatever the level of our own need (Matthew 15:22-28).

Now then, what will an awesome deed in righteousness look like in your life? Go ahead and dream and pray big – you cannot possibly out dream God or ask too much of Him!

Now glory be to God! By His mighty power at work within us, He is able to accomplish infinitely more than we would ever dare to ask or hope.

EPHESIANS 3:20 NLT

Coming soon – Awesome deeds in righteousness

What is in store for the world in the coming days? Even the worst of what we have experienced in life to this point will fade from our memory by the coming terrible and awesome deeds in righteousness! The earth will continue her revulsion at man's sinfulness and evil[7]. In fact, such horrors will only increase in both frequency and intensity.

However, the Church of Jesus Christ is in for her finest moments! Entire nations will repent and come to Christ in a day! This last flurry of activity will take our breath away! Believers who catch this revelation will fulfill the prophecy of Jesus to "do greater works than these" (John 14:12). These concluding moments will be just that: mere moments as time races to its final conclusion and its last meeting with the Ancient of Days, the Alpha and Omega, the I AM that I AM!

The Church's closing moments will be the most awesome moments in history as we race to win the last of the last souls coming to Christ. Until at that moments' arrival when the final soul is gathered safely in, the definitive awesome deed in righteousness will be manifest for the entire world to see. Maybe we should say, not see "for in a twinkling of an eye" the Bride of Christ will be caught up to meet the Lord in the air! Yes, the final awesome deed in righteousness that we will experience here on the earth will be the Blessed Hope, the Rapture of the Church! And so shall we ever be with the Lord!

"Maranatha! Even so, come Lord Jesus!"

The Essence – "Pray for the season of Aaron's Rod"[8] There is a change of seasons coming upon the earth. We, the whole body of Christ, will soon be experiencing the full manifestation of the glory of God in unprecedented ways! The Spirit will confirm His voice through His people and we will experience at once supernatural growth, budding, blooming and fruit – every season visible in a moment! The harvesters will overtake the sowers as we gather this last great harvest of souls before the return of Jesus Christ! And with this fresh season will also come the judgment of the rebellious nations of the world.

nine

THE SEASON OF AARON'S ROD

GOD ORDAINS THE seasons! There is something in the air! The season is changing.

For, lo, the winter is past, the rain is over and gone; the flowers appear on the earth; the time of the singing of birds is come, and the voice of the turtledove is heard in our land; the fig tree puts forth her green figs, and the vines with the tender grape give a good smell. Arise, my love, my fair one, and come away.

SONG OF SOLOMON 2:11-13

The Church is entering her final moments of world history, and these hours will be her finest! Before us lies the greatest opportunity for world evangelism that the people of God have ever witnessed. The knowledge of the glory of God is covering the earth, and His fame is intensifying among the peoples.

There is an appointed time for everything. And there is a time for every event under heaven.

ECCLESIASTES 3:1 NASB

The Event of the Ages is about to commence as Jesus returns for His Church with the cry,

"Arise, My love, My fair one, and come away!"

SONG OF SOLOMON 2:13

We may desire a different season in life or reminisce about better times, but ultimately the seasons of our lives and ministries, as the seasons of nature, are in God's hand!

And He changes the times and the seasons. He removes kings, and sets up kings. He gives wisdom unto the wise, and knowledge to them that know understanding.

DANIEL 2:21

We may labor long and hard, pursue the finest education and the latest technological advances, hire the best administrators and staff, but the ultimate determining factor in life's success is the ability to hear the voice of the Lord and subsequently move with His Spirit.

My times are in Your hand...

Ps.ALM31:15

The spirit of anti-Christ attempts to change the seasons

All those who attempt to enter the Kingdom of God by any method or means other than by the door, Jesus Christ, have been identified and Jesus has identified them as thieves.

Verily, verily, I say unto you, he that enters not by the door into the sheepfold, but climbs up some other way, the same is a thief and a robber.

JOHN 10:1

How many people attempt to change, not necessarily the way, but the time? There is no difference, whether we endeavor to enter the Kingdom by a different door than Christ, or by a different time other than His, all those entering illegally, will be branded as thieves!

One of the characteristics of the spirit of the anti-Christ will be the arrogance to believe that changing the times and season is within his power.

And he shall speak great words against the Most High, and shall wear out the saints of the Most High, and think to change times and laws: and they shall be given into his hand until a time and times and the dividing of time.

DANIEL 7:25

As in all the tactics of the evil one, his most potent weapons against the saints are his deceptions – "has God said?" Once we lose our basis for life and faith – the Word of God – we become vulnerable to Satan's even more subtle work of wearing down the saints. This should never be, for Satan's weapons are merely natural or carnal in nature, while the saint has at his disposal — supernatural weapons.

> *For though we walk in the flesh, we do not war after the flesh: (For the weapons of our warfare are not carnal, but mighty through God to the pulling down of strong holds)...*
>
> 2 CORINTHIANS 10:3-4

While the devil may attempt to cause us to "grow weary in well doing" (see Galatians 6:9; 2 Thessalonians 3:13) thus tripping us up and hoping to keep us from our destiny, we hold weapons of faith and patience that when once used will manifest the promises of God.

> *For ye have need of patience, that, after ye have done the will of God, ye might receive the promise. For yet a little while, and He that shall come will come, and will not tarry. Now the just shall live by faith: but if any man draws back, My soul shall have no pleasure in him. But we are not of them who draw back unto perdition; but of them that believe to the saving of the soul.*
>
> HEBREWS 10:36-39

It is in this hour that the believing Church must arise and be found in a living and vital faith, which will facilitate our vigilance and anticipation for the coming of the Lord Jesus!

> *...Nevertheless when the Son of man cometh, shall He find faith on the earth?*
>
> LUKE 18:8

An effective spiritual weapon carried by all Christians but most often overlooked is the supernatural character of Christ – the fruit of the Spirit being born within our lives.

> *But the fruit of the Spirit is ...longsuffering...*
>
> GALATIANS 5:22-23

Without a doubt, we have the ability in Christ alone to outlast any assault of the wicked one for we have an infinite supply of Jesus' patient endurance! Now, while the devil may attempt to thwart our progress, if we persevere we are assured to experience the Lord's victory!

As this spirit of anti-Christ strives to thwart us (see 1 Thessalonians 2:18; Daniel 7:25), in attempting to divert the seasons ordained by God and thereby causing us to doubt God's Word, we are only in danger of experiencing incomplete victory, if we faint.

And let us not be weary in well doing: for in due season we shall reap, if we faint not.

GALATIANS 6:9

You see, there is an appointed time for the harvest (Genesis 8:22)! Our job is to remain faithful to Kingdom purposes, guard our hearts and faith, obey the promptings of the Holy Spirit and wait on the Lord. We must also demonstrate our faith by our actions and our faithful service to the people of God as well as those in need of the Gospel. The season of victory will come as we take this aggressive posture in intercession. As we unite with the Holy Spirit's prayers we will be found awaiting the victory, and that, right on the front row!

Hearing the Word of the Lord

When the word of the Christ comes to us, it can often catch us off guard. We may be so focused on a specific thought or purpose – a specific mindset – that when He speaks to us it will often cut perpendicularly across all we have had in mind or expected. And yet, it will always bear the unmistakable earmarks of the peace and wisdom of Christ (Philippians 4:7; Colossians 3:15; James 3:17-18).

One such hearing of a verse, Psalm 102:13, it is one of those verses that many in the Church have laid hold of to wage a good spiritual warfare for Israel and her Ending Days restoration; and rightly so.

"You shall arise, and have mercy upon Zion: for the time to favour her, yes, the set time, is come."

PSALM 102:13

The appointed time has come for the ancient people of God! The time has come for Israel and the descendants of Abraham to see the Messiah's glory, to have the veil removed from their eyes that they might see...

"And I will pour out on the house of David and on the inhabitants of Jerusalem, the Spirit of grace and of supplication, so that they will look

on Me whom they have pierced; and they will mourn for Him, as one mourns for an only son, and they will weep bitterly over Him, like the bitter weeping over a first-born."

.ZECHARIAH 12:10 NASB

But, Psalm 102:13 is not just for the Jew. It is also for the believing Church. This blessing is for Zion, the collective peoples of God!⁹ This is the allotted time for the final culmination of Yahweh's purposes in the earth through His People.

It was while I was praying and meditating on this verse ""You shall arise, and have mercy upon Zion: for the time to favour her, yes, the set time, is come", that there came the crystal clear clarity of the Spirit speaking into my heart. He said, "Pray for the season of Aaron's Rod."¹⁰

Most assuredly we have come to that time in history where all is in readiness for the Second Coming of the Lord Jesus Christ. Yes, it is time for the changing of seasons and it is time now for the season of Aaron's Rod!

Aaron's Rod

It was just a stick! Some refreshing of our memories may be helpful. Yes, maybe it was just a walking stick, an ordinary stick – a stick to support yourself as you walk through the loose rock and sand of the desert. It was also a valuable aid to defend against animals or serpents. Most likely, in addition to these roles of support and defense, it became something of the family genealogical record as well and hence, a symbol of authority. While tending the herds and flocks of the family, during those times of personal quiet and reflection, the opportunity may have been taken to use a knife and carve a narrative of the family's history — a prompter for the oral history every child must memorize. From top to bottom it may have been carved with important family names, key patriarchs of the family... Abraham, Isaac, Jacob. Levi. Critical events that impacted the family – maybe the ram that Yahweh provided in Abraham's son, Isaac's stead, or the ladder of Jacob's dream might have been found inscribed upon such a stick. But still, it was just a stick, even if it had meaning, as was still just an ordinary stick! And it is wise for us to remember too that our faith must be applied to any and all points of life lest things merely become empty traditions, lifeless rituals, or the delusion that we have somehow gained wealth, blessing, and position in our own strength.

Who's got the real goods?

In Numbers 16 we find the judgment of Korah and the murmuring of the people. Their offenses were jealousy and the arrogance to believe that they too should have the right to offer sacrifice before Yahweh. Actually, this was the initial intent of the Lord — to have a "holy nation of priests" but the Jewish nation rejected the Lord's offer!

And ye shall be unto Me a kingdom of priests, and an holy nation.
Exodus 19:6

But ye are a chosen generation, a royal priesthood, an holy nation, a peculiar people; that ye should show forth the praises of Him who hath called you out of darkness into Hs marvelous light.
1 Peter 2:9

How many Christians today are still rejecting the Lord's gracious offer? Even so, rebellion is never the proper way to appropriate spiritual principles and realize the fullness of Kingdom life in our families and churches.

The test

To meet this challenge of God's appointed authorities in the priesthood, the Lord instructs Moses to gather every tribal leader's rod or staff. Once assembled, they were to place them in the Tabernacle. By the morning's light, God would have spoken convincingly about His sovereign choice for the priesthood.

The next day Moses entered the Tent of the Testimony and saw that Aaron's staff, which represented the house of Levi, had not only sprouted but had budded, blossomed and produced almonds.
Numbers 17:8 NIV

Think about it... every season in a moment! Every aspect of life had manifest in a single instant! This stick, this old dead stick had grown new green branches! It had also sprouted fresh green leaves. Not only that, but overnight it had produced fragrant blossoms and amazingly even ripe almonds! Yes, the Lord had spoken! All could see, touch, smell, and taste the miracle! Every season was present at once – from the dormancy of winter to the abundance of the autumn harvest!

What will this season of Aaron's Rod look like?

Some are already experiencing the beginnings of this new Season! Others are awakening to this season of Aaron's Rod and as they do, they will find themselves overtaken by the blessings of God – caught off guard by the goodness of the Lord!

As surely as the Body of Christ is expecting,

> *...nation to rise against nation, and kingdom against kingdom: and there shall be famines, and pestilences, and earthquakes, in many places of the earth*
>
> MATTHEW 24:7

So we need to begin to understand that while the earth is in the midst of birthing a new Kingdom, so we should be expecting a supernatural moving of God's Spirit!

> *"The time will come," says the LORD, "When the grain and grapes will grow faster than they can be harvested. Then the terraced vineyards on the hills of Israel will drip with sweet wine!"*
>
> AMOS 9:13 NLT

The King James Version says it this way,

> *"Behold, the days come", saith the LORD, "That the plowman shall overtake the reaper, and the treader of grapes him that sows seed; and the mountains shall drop sweet wine, and all the hills shall melt."*

Amazing - in the coming moments of time just before the Lord's return you will barely get the seed in the ground before your harvest will manifest! The reapers will be on the heels of the sowers who will be pressing them to increase their speed and encouraging them to sow faster and in greater measure! As the instant and miraculous results manifest before all to see, the sowers will pick up the pace and in a matter of days or weeks the precious harvest of the peoples of the earth will be complete!! The invitation to receive Christ may not even be given before the repentant seekers are at the altars. The services will not even begin before the lost are finding mercy at the Throne of Grace. Before you begin to pray for your lost co-workers, they will be searching you out asking if you will pray for them to become Christians, "What must we do to be saved" (see Acts 2:37; 16:30, Zechariah 8:23)? Signs and wonders will accompany and announce the presence of God in our homes, churches and city streets! Crowded mega-stores will become holy sites as the miraculous breaks out in the aisles! "Lift up your heads," the season of Aaron's Rod is upon us!

> *And it shall come to pass, if you shall hearken diligently unto the voice of the LORD thy God, to observe and to do all His commandments which I command you this day, that the LORD thy God will set you on high above all nations of the earth: and all these blessings shall come on you, and overtake you, if you shall hearken unto the voice of the LORD your God.*
>
> DEUTERONOMY 28:1-2

The Lord has spoken, and as the budding of Aaron's Rod gave attestation to His chosen priesthood, so the Spirit of God's verification of the message of the Gospel will be seen in and on those believers who are daring enough to believe the Gospel and act upon it! The authority of Jesus will find a daring and bold breed of believers who, clothed at once with His humility, authority, and power that is even now advancing the Gospel at an unprecedented rate!

> *"Go ye into all the world, and preach the Gospel to every creature. He that believeth and is baptized shall be saved; but he that believeth not shall be damned. And these signs shall follow them that believe; In My name shall they cast out devils; they shall speak with new tongues; They shall take up serpents; and if they drink any deadly thing, it shall not hurt them; they shall lay hands on the sick, and they shall recover." So then after the Lord had spoken unto them, He was received up into heaven, and sat on the right hand of God. And they went forth, and preached every where, the Lord working with them, and confirming the Word with signs following. Amen.*
>
> MARK 16: 15-20

The Season of Aaron's Rod and the Jewish People

The initial miracle of Aaron's Rod came about as an attestation of God's divinely appointed authority over His people. The Lord had chosen and appointed Moses as their leader, and Aaron along with his sons were appointed to the priesthood. These appointments were challenged to the point of rebellion and civil war (Numbers 16). God answered in dramatic fashion. He had spoken, and now He would confirm His appointed and anointed leaders (Numbers 17:8). Whether in Moses' day or in ours we must face this issue of man's rebellion and his defiance of God's leadership and the questioning of His wisdom concerning His rightful governing over our lives!

It is no different today. Israel's very right to exist among the family of nations is being challenged. The nation of Israel, as well as the Jewish people scattered among the nations, is experiencing a worldwide surge in anti-Semitism. Palestinian suicide bombers, nuclear and biological weapons, Middle Eastern Islamic nations, a hostile and irrational United Nations, and violent anti-Semitic gangs throughout Europe have all sided to defiantly and arrogantly challenge the right of the Jewish people to their God-given land and destiny. This evil intent has as its goal the total and final annihilation of every Jew and with them the rule of God. This is Satan's concluding attempt at his last and grandest "final solution." It is his final assault on the integrity and purity of God's Word.

Even as the Lord defended and vindicated Moses and Aaron — a modern day Rod of Aaron is about to be revealed among the nations of the earth as Yahweh stands up to confirm and defend His ancient people, not to mention His Son's Bride, the Church. Jesus, the Rod of Aaron, "the rod out of Jesse" will settle the issue once and for all. Messiah will reign, establishing forever His righteous government.

And there shall come forth a rod out of the stem of Jesse, and a Branch shall grow out of His roots: and the Spirit of the LORD shall rest upon Him, the spirit of wisdom and understanding, the spirit of counsel and might, the spirit of knowledge and of the fear of the LORD; and shall make Him of quick understanding in the fear of the LORD: and He shall not judge after the sight of His eyes, neither reprove after the hearing of His ears: but with righteousness shall He judge the poor, and reprove with equity for the meek of the earth: and He shall smite the earth with the rod of His mouth, and with the breath of His lips shall

Mark D. Spencer

He slay the wicked. And righteousness shall be the girdle of His loins, and faithfulness the girdle of His reins.
ISAIAH 11:1-5; (ALSO SEE JEREMIAH 3:17; MICAH 4:1-3; ZECHARIAH 8:22; 12:9; 14:16)

The Season of Aaron's Rod and the nations

The manifestation of Aaron's Rod initially was a judgment of Yahweh upon the rebellious leaders and usurpers who had intent to remove Moses and Aaron (the LORD's chosen and appointed leaders) and substitute themselves as the rulers over God's people Israel (Numbers 16). Their arrogance and the subsequent assertion that they could stand in an office of God's appointment without His anointing brought quick and horrible judgment, not only on themselves but on their families as well.

While the manifestation of Aaron's Rod will bring untold blessing to the body of Christ along with the attestation that we are the called and anointed of God, so it will bring speedy judgment to those who continue to deny and resist the Lordship of Jesus Christ!

The king proclaims the Lord's decree: the LORD said to Me, "You are My son. Today I have become your Father. Only ask, and I will give You the nations as Your inheritance, the ends of the earth as Your possession. You will break them with an iron rod and smash them like clay pots." Now then, you kings, act wisely! Be warned, you rulers of the earth! Serve the LORD with reverent fear, and rejoice with trembling. Submit to God's royal Son, or He will become angry, and you will be destroyed in the midst of your pursuits - for His anger can flare up in an instant. But what joy for all who find protection in Him!
PSALM 2:7-12 NLT

As the Master has taught us to pray for our enemies so we begin to see why there is a vital and practical reason for it. When challenged, Moses and Aaron, in falling on their faces to both mark their humility and their intercession for the people, give us a clear example that we too are called to pray for our enemies lest they fall under our Father's righteous judgment!

But I say unto you, "Love your enemies, bless them that curse you, do good to them that hate you, and pray for them which despitefully use you, and persecute you; that ye may be the children of your Father which is in heaven..."

MATTHEW 5:44 – 45

Are there people for whom you need to pray for today, speaking forgiveness and mercy over their lives, blessing them and not cursing?

A new season of Ending Day's financial harvest

Some may scoff at this new season, but for those who have given of their all to the proclamation of the Gospel there will also come a reaping in the financial realm of unprecedented magnitude! This final season of Aaron's Rod will not be confined to the salvation of men from their sins alone, but will also demonstrate the Lord's ability to redeem and restore their fortunes as well.

> *I will be found by you, says the LORD. I will end your captivity and restore your fortunes.*

JEREMIAH 29:14

The season of the release of the Ending Day's financial outpouring is upon us! Simply put, it takes vast sums of money to take the message of Jesus' deliverance and salvation to the ends of the earth. The only harvest in these Ending Days more miraculous than the financial harvest will be the harvest of souls in these closing moments of history!

The call to enduring prayer

> *And when they cried unto the LORD, He put darkness between you and the Egyptians, and brought the sea upon them, and covered them; and your eyes have seen what I have done in Egypt: and ye dwelt in the wilderness a long season.*

JOSHUA 24:7

When days turn into months and months into years, it can be easy to "grow weary in well doing." But we must persevere for the alternatives are unacceptable. While it rarely seems that the spring and autumn seasons are long enough, the seasons of winter or summer often tend to drag on and on. The cold or the heat gives the appearance that it will never end. There is a longing for the freshness of the spring's warmth or the crisp of autumn's cool. While spiritual seasons cannot be calculated on a calendar as can the seasons of nature, they are just as real and their change inevitable!

While the purposes and plans of God will come to completion on time and uninterrupted by the devises of devils or schemes of men, believing Christians do have an important part to play in their fulfillment.

> *You should look forward to that Day and hurry it along - the day when God will set the heavens on fire and the elements will melt away in the flames.*
>
> 2 PETER 3:12 NLT

The prophet Daniel, being a man of prayer, saw the purpose of God for the return of the Jew to Jerusalem from their captivity in Babylon. Many today would offer a glib "praise the Lord" and go about their daily business. Not Daniel, he began to take hold of these promises and allow the Holy Spirit a channel in which to believe for the fulfillment of Jeremiah's prophecies. Paul saw the importance of the Jewish people in the Ending Days and made intercession accordingly.

> *Brethren, my heart's desire and prayer to God for Israel is that they might be saved.*
>
> ROMANS 10:1

Other saints throughout history have seen God's purposes for their generation and joined His labor of intercession — travailing in spiritual birth until that thing was accomplished, or they had the witness that they had finished their part in its completion by prayer and faith.

> *For David, after he had served the purpose of God in his own generation, fell asleep.*
>
> ACTS 13:36 NASB

Never give up your stand of intercession nor your place in intercession until the Lord releases you from the assignment!

Waiting in faith

As we are laboring in intercession and while we are waiting in faith the manifestation of this "Season of Aaron's Rod", our responsibility as believers is to be constant regardless of the season we are currently experiencing. Remember, it is God's responsibility to change the seasons. However, if we have devotedly accomplished our assignment, then we will be ready to experience the entirety of the Lord's best as the season does change. We must be poised in our spirits having proven ourselves in consistently abiding in the Word of God and in faithful ministry to the Lord and His people.

> *Preach the Word; be instant in season, out of season; reprove, rebuke, exhort with all longsuffering and doctrine.*
>
> 2 TIMOTHY 4:2

We may not yield to the temptations to become lax in our intercessions, but press through until we have obtained the desired promise.

> *But oh, my dear children! I feel as if I am going through labor pains for you again, and they will continue until Christ is fully developed in your lives.*
>
> GALATIANS 4:19 NLT

Time not wasted

Our time spent in believing prayer is never wasted time.

> *"The time will come," says the LORD, "When the grain and grapes will grow faster than they can be harvested. Then the terraced vineyards on the hills of Israel will drip with sweet wine!"*
>
> AMOS 9:13 NLT

It is an interesting fact of nature that the longer a grape remains upon the vine, the sweeter it becomes as its starches are being converted to sugars. This long stay upon the vine—even to the point of withering – produces the sweetest of the wines. From the famed Chateau Barrosa, in the Barrosa Valley wine district of South Australia, they have this to say about their Late Pick Frontignac wine, "This wine realizes the huge potential of the white Frontignac grape, which is harvested after the vine leaves have dropped and the berries begin to shrivel, thus intensifying the flavors and sugar content. The result is a floral bouquet with a generous palate and an elegant firm finish."

For many Christians it may seem the harvest is past and the leaves have fallen from their branches. The season is over and all they can see is a withered and wasted or fruitless life. Even the Harvester seems to have passed them over, and any fruit in their lives appears to have been rejected or over-looked. Possibly it may be gathered for use by a few poor and beggarly gleaners, but mostly left for the fowl of the air or the beasts of the field. Even if this may seem the case for your life, it is not the Master's plan. For those who have experienced a long dry season or a hard period where your labors have gone seemingly unnoticed, and maybe you are at the place where you feel you are about ready to expire, to wither away, or to faint in your well doing – you must understand this, this is the moment for which the Lord has been working! Surely it has been unperceivable to you, but He has been perfecting the character and nature of Jesus Christ within your life.

> *For I reckon that the sufferings of this present time are not worthy to be compared with the glory which shall be revealed in us. For the earnest expectation of the creation waits for the manifestation of the sons of God.*
>
> ROMANS 8:18-19

Your character is growing sweeter and sweeter. The fruits of the Spirit within your heart are becoming riper and riper. Those to whom the Lord is sending you – whether family or friends, co-workers or neighbors, peoples or nations, the fragrance and aroma of your life is becoming more and more attractive, all the while pointing to the goodness of the Lord. Be confident therefore in Christ's aroma of life at work within you.

> *O taste and see that the LORD is good: blessed is the man that trusts in Him.*
>
> PSALM 34:8

Through this hard and difficult time there is a message of His life fermenting and being prepared within your life. And it is this message and fruit which He intends to serve to those in need of the Saviour!

> *Usually a host serves the best wine first, he said. Then, when everyone is full and doesn't care, he brings out the less expensive wines. But you have kept the best until now!*
>
> JOHN 2:10

Be encouraged, the Lord has kept the best wine – the best fruit, until now!

...who knows whether you are come to the kingdom for such a time as this?

ESTHER 4:14

The change is in the wind

And Jesus also said to the people, "When you see a cloud rise out of the west, straightway you say, There cometh a shower; and so it is. And when ye see the south wind blow, ye say, there will be heat; and it cometh to pass. Ye hypocrites, ye can discern the face of the sky and of the earth; but how is it that ye do not discern this time?"

LUKE 12:54-56

It seems every season has its unique and peculiar winds. It might be said that the seasons change on the winds. And so as we anticipate the changing of the seasons and wait with increasing expectancy for the coming of the season of Aaron's Rod, so we must look to the Wind!

And suddenly there came a sound from heaven as of a rushing mighty wind, and it filled all the house where they were sitting.

ACTS 2:2

Jesus is Master of all nature as well as Lord of time. He is the Lord of the Harvest and He is also the Master of the Wind!

But the men marveled, saying, 'What manner of man is this, that even the winds and the sea obey Him!'

MATTHEW 8:27

These winds of change and winds of the seasons obey the voice of Jesus. They bring the visitations of God's Spirit and pour forth the necessary rains of revival and restoration. From His abundant storehouse and provision the Lord meets the needs of the people.

Mark D. Spencer

When He speaks, there is thunder in the heavens. He causes the clouds to rise over the earth. He sends the lightning with the rain and releases the wind from His storehouses.

JEREMIAH 10:13

As Jesus challenged His disciples so He is challenging us today to believe Him for the outpouring of this Ending Day season of Aaron's Rod. Faith is required. Faith is demanded. Faith is necessary if we are to see the completion of the age and witness the return of Christ. Faith's demand will produce the desired result!

And He said unto them, 'Where is your faith?' And they, being afraid wondered, saying one to another, 'What manner of man is this! For He commands even the winds and water, and they obey Him.'

LUKE 8:25

"Speak to the wind!"

We are called to give utterance to His voice – the voice of faith – calling for the winds to change the season and bring this last great visitation of the Spirit of God to the earth. Our prophetic intercession and ministries will be empowered by the Lord of the Harvest as He mobilizes this Ending Days army of evangelists and apostolic ministry.

Then He said to me, "Speak to the winds and say: 'This is what the Sovereign LORD says: 'Come, O breath, from the four winds! Breathe into these dead bodies so that they may live again.'" So I spoke as He commanded me, and the wind entered the bodies, and they began to breathe. They all came to life and stood up on their feet - a great army of them.

EZEKIEL 37:9-10

Over the gardens and fields that are white unto harvest there will blow the gentile winds of God's Spirit wooing and calling the lost to "taste and see that the Lord is good" (Psalm 34:8). So prophesy now with the Preacher,

Awake, O north wind; and come, thou south wind; blow upon My garden (My Church), that the spices thereof may flow out. Let My beloved (the

lost of the world) come into His garden, and eat His pleasant fruits (salvation's blessings).
SONG OF SOLOMON 4:16

In this Ending Day's season of Aaron's Rod, we may expect the Lord's supernatural manifestations quickly. Things will change for us overnight, suddenly, and often spectacularly!

What should we expect in this season of Aaron's Rod? Watch for a victorious and triumphant Church. Watch for increase and provision, favor and reproduction on every front! Believers will be living radical lives for Christ (and many will give their all for His sake). We will see those miraculous things in the Church that we have longed to see. We will also see these mighty signs and wonders in the most foundational aspect of the Church and that is in the lives of those individual's who have been laboring in prayer and intercession for the glory of God to fall. These faithful intercessors may be the first to realize this season in their own lives. To expect the miraculous within the Church is to expect it in your personal life. Those who have been laboring in their prayer closets, believing for the breaking out of this Ending Days season, will see the same increase and provision, favor and reproduction that they have been expecting and believing for within the Church.

Can you see why it is important for you to be in a Spirit-filled, faith and love filled local church? For what we are believing for within our local churches may well be that which we may also expect to find manifested in our personal lives! It is scriptural therefore, to expect God's increase in both your life and your church's corporate life, for the Kingdom of God is a kingdom of increase.

The LORD shall increase you more and more, you and your children.
PSALM 115:14

Of the increase of His government and peace there shall be no end.
ISAIAH 9:7

Expect God's provision in your life, for the Father has made ample provision for His children and His people.

God is able to make all grace abound to you, so that in all things at all times, having all that you need, you will abound in every good work.
2 CORINTHIANS 9:8

Expect God's favor upon your life for it is the evidence of His good hand of blessing being upon your life.

And let the beauty and delightfulness and favor of the Lord our God be upon us; confirm and establish the work of our hands - yes, the work of our hands, confirm and establish it.

PSALM 90:17 AMPLIFIED

Expect Life's reproduction to be upon you and within you. It is the nature of life to beget more life after its own kind. How much more then will the Zoë life of God, which is at work within you, create within you His Zoë life (Genesis 1).

Herein is My Father glorified, that you bear much fruit; so shall you be My disciples.

JOHN 15:8

It is God's desire that all those people that the Spirit brings into our lives be recipients of the blessing we carry. This is the mark we bear of Christ's life within us that His life radiates out to others through us.

Every detail works to our advantage and to God's glory, more and more grace, more and more people, more and more praise.

2 CORINTHIANS 4:15 THE MESSAGE

Expect the breaking loose of the season of Aaron's Rod. Yes, expect God to act by His Spirit. Faith always stretches out. You may have prayed and prayed for something, but at some point, faith calls you to reach out and begin believing beyond the present circumstances of your life. Faith sees the end from the beginning. Expectant faith sees the result before the manifestation. Faith lays claim to the promises of God as all the evidence necessary to jumpstart your rejoicing. This isn't about foolish or presumptive prayers, but rather prayers that yesterday may have seemed impossible, but today are grasped and obtainable in Christ. Your prayers offered today in faith, will become the realities of your life tomorrow.

I will answer them before they even call to Me. While they are still talking to me about their needs, I will go ahead and answer their prayers!

ISAIAH 65: 24

Expectant faith continues to stand, continues to believe, and continues to persevere regardless of the season for it knows that a new season is coming – and that at any moment! It's in the air!

"Pray for the season of Aaron's Rod."

The Essence – The book of Revelation teaches us that there are various prayer bowls in heaven that must be filled with faithful and believing prayer before the answer to those prayers can be released. We are called to be "faithful, faithful, faithful..." before we can experience the "fruit" of these prayers. Further, we are called to be in the right place at the right time in the right frame (or right "faith frame") of mind, so that our prayers can be answered! Having been faithful in importunate prayer we will be positioned to receive the answers to our faith!

ten

"Faithful... Faithful... Faithful... Fruit!"

God is faithful, by whom ye were called unto the fellowship of His Son Jesus Christ our Lord.

1 Corinthians 1:9

The PRAYER OF IMPORTUNITY IS an often forgotten spiritual weapon that is critical to the believer's success. In life we must learn how to exercise this specific type of intercessory prayer so that our prayer bowls may be filled to overflowing and we may experience the glory of God as He answers faithful intercession.

And Jesus said unto them, "Which of you that has a friend who has come to you at midnight, and said, 'Friend, lend me three loaves of bread; for a friend of mine in his journey is come to me, and I have nothing to set before him?' And then he said from within his house, 'Don't trouble me: the door is now shut, and my children are with me in bed; I cannot rise and help you.' So I say unto you, though he will not rise and help him, even though he is his friend, yet because of his importunity he will rise and give him as much as he needs." "And I say unto you, ask, and it shall be given you; seek, and ye shall find; knock, and it shall be opened unto you. For every one that asks receives and he that seeks finds; and to him that knocks it shall be opened."

Luke 11:5-10

While teaching this message overseas, I came to the word "importunity" and it proved to be one of those words that caused my translator an awkward moment. Indeed, importunity is one of those old, yet specific English words that have fallen out of modern usage – probably because we no longer want to hear of anything that has to do with persistence or pertinacity. Pertinacity by the way, is; "a firm or unyielding adherence to opinion or purpose." In a world that has made gods of "relevance", "political correctness", and so called "tolerance," the virtues of truth and persistence and character building have suffered immeasurable damage! Before we begin to look into what the Word of God holds for us concerning the prayer of importunity, maybe it would be good for us to define the word importunity. Importunity is, "the pressing solicitation, an urgent request; an application for a claim or favor, which is urged with troublesome frequency or pertinacity" (Webster's 1828 Edition).

And what of this word importunity and the modern Church world? Could it be that we too often expect immediacy to our spirituality in the same manner as we do in all aspects of living – from fast food to weight loss without exercise, from get rich schemes to empty self-oriented relationships? We want and demand all of our desires to be granted immediately! Yes, there is the "suddenly" of the moving of God's Spirit and we should wait upon Him with a confident expectation and joyful anticipation of such "suddenlies" of His breaking into our lives. But to be quite candid, most "suddenlies" are built upon a life of consistency and faithfulness! One highly successful man of God when asked how his ministry seemed to blossom overnight responded "that overnight was the longest 20 years of my life!" With this understanding, we can see that it is very important that we not shy away from such values should the words themselves become outdated. Such is often our culture's dupability; to give as little effort as possible but in return demand that we receive as much back as possible! We might say it this way, "Give us fruit, fruit and more fruit, and if we must, we will offer as little character or faithfulness as possible in return." As with most truths, the Kingdom of God's view is diametrically opposed to such humanistic and selfish worldviews!

"Faithful... faithful... faithful... fruit!"

Character development is never easy. There are never any three-step formulas for molding character within the human heart. Jesus stated the condition of Christian maturity when He said,

> *If you abide (continue) in My Word, then you are truly disciples of Mine; and you shall know the truth, and the truth shall make you free.*
> JOHN 8:31-32

It has been said the Christian life is a long obedience in the same direction.[11] In matters of temporal things the world understands these principles.

One only needs to look to the devotion of the Olympian to his sport to see this dedication and determination. This commitment is either for the pure love of the sport or to have an opportunity to win a fleeting honor. Sadly, it is the character traits of godliness and inner moral strength that are glossed over for more convenient and quicker routes to spiritual "fulfillment." This is why we can have a nation of religious yet immoral, spiritual yet empty people!

A peek into the unseen

The book of Revelation offers us a glimpse into the prayer of importunity. Without an understanding of such prayer we may find ourselves confused and even discouraged when we are attempting to offer a prayer of faith in place of the prayer of importunity. As a carpenter's tool belt holds various tools – "there is a right tool for every job" – so there are tools in the Christian's prayer "tool belt" that must be used if we are to have a successful and powerful life of prayer! There is the prayers of agreement, the prayers of faith, the prayers of confession, the prayers of binding and loosing and so forth.

We should clarify at the onset that all prayer, if it is to please God and obtain answers from Him, must be offered in faith! Without faith, you simply cannot please God!

So, you see, it is impossible to please God without faith. Anyone who wants to come to Him must believe that there is a God and that He rewards those who sincerely seek Him.
HEBREWS 11:6 NLT

Without faith, your prayer no matter how sincere, no matter how tearful, no matter how long, is just so many empty religious mutterings and idle, inoperative non-working words! Such words find no audience but the ceiling of the room in which they were uttered.

But I tell you, on the day of judgment men will have to give account for every idle (inoperative, nonworking) word they speak.
MATTHEW 12:36 AMPLIFIED

Filling our prayer bowls

And when He had taken the book, the four living creatures and the twenty-four elders fell down before the Lamb, having each one a harp, and golden bowls full of incense, which are the prayers of the saints.
REVELATION 5:8 NASB

We can see from John's eyewitness account that there are bowls in heaven – golden bowls, which hold the prayers of the saints! While we cannot be dogmatic about this, it is not hard to construe that there may be various bowls for individuals, churches, and even nations. These bowls, when full, release the desired answer upon the earth.

And we further read in the book of Revelation,

And another angel came and stood at the altar, holding a golden censer; and much incense was given to him, that he might add it to the prayers of all the saints upon the golden altar which was before the throne. And the smoke of the incense, with the prayers of the saints, went up before God out of the angel's hand. And the angel took the censer; and he filled it with the fire of the altar and threw it to the earth; and there followed peals of thunder and sounds and flashes of lightning and an earthquake.
REVELATION 8:3-5 NASB

There may be nothing more thrilling than having a specific answer to prayer. When the Living God acts in response to a prayer offered in confident faith it is one of the most dynamic of spiritual experiences. Indeed it is electrifying. Such answers may rightfully be called the "thunderings and lightnings of God!"

As these prayer bowls are filled with prayer that has been offered in faith we see an amazing thing transpire. An angel from the presence of God brings a censer filled with fire and adds it to the bowls of prayer. It is after this fire from the altar of God is added to the bowls that they are then hurled to the earth. This hurling of the prayer bowl to the earth clearly signifies the answer to prayers that the saints have been waiting for – the manifestation in this natural realm of what has been diligently believed for and "seen" by the eye of faith while in prayer and intercession. Faith obtains in the now what cannot be seen with the natural eye or discerned by the natural senses.

"Faithful... faithful... faithful... fruit!"

Filling our prayer bowls—the practical working.

Nothing is better on a cold Colorado winter's day than a bowl of rich, steaming soup full of fresh vegetables, hearty meat, and savory broth! No one likes a watery and weak broth made with scant few vegetables and poor cuts of meat. Soup without rich substance is a meager gruel, satisfying neither palate nor stomach! And yet when it comes to prayer most believers spend their time filling their prayer bowls with weak or non-existent faith mingled with emotional pleas, human opinion, murmurings and complaints. Such prayer is nothing more than a lukewarm spiritual pottage! Strong confidence and vibrant faith based upon the Word of God mixed with heartfelt praise produces overflowing answers from the Throne of God!

"Faithful... faithful... faithful... fruit!"

It may be that some prayer bowls are larger than others and so demand more intense prayer, greater patient endurance in prayer, united prayer, or forgiving prayer. Whatever the situation we are facing, the Lord desires to answer prayer to the end we might be blessed, other people be blessed, and His Son glorified (John 14:14; 15:7; 16:23-26).

> *And He spoke a parable unto them to this end, that men ought always to pray, and not to faint; saying, there was in a city a judge, which feared not God, neither regarded man: and there was a widow in that city; and she came unto him, saying, avenge me of mine adversary. And he would not for a while: but afterward he said within himself, 'Though I fear not God, nor regard man; yet because this widow troubles me, I will avenge her, lest by her continual coming she weary me.' And the Lord said, 'Hear what the unjust judge says. And shall not God avenge His own elect, which cry day and night unto Him, though He bear long with them? I tell you that He will avenge them speedily. Nevertheless when the Son of man cometh, shall He find faith on the earth?'*
>
> LUKE 18:1-8

"Faithful... faithful... faithful... fruit!"

A contrast not a comparison!

Jesus is not comparing the unjust judge to God the Righteous Judge and His righteous judgments; rather He is contrasting the goodness and rightness of God's judgments to the wicked and injustice of the unjust judge. And so the contrast is invoked to encourage the believer, who aware of the goodness and rightness of God's character and mercy, may be confident that the heart of God can be persuaded far easier and moved far quicker than the arguments needed to convince an unjust and stubborn judge to act on their behalf! This parable is designed to stir hope in the believer's heart as well as release our faith for answers to our prayers. "... shall not God?"

"*Faithful... faithful... faithful... fruit!*"

Defining our words

Because words are containers conveying ideas and the contents of man's heart, it becomes crucial that we use precise words to convey as accurately as possible those thoughts. Defining words that may give us trouble or confuse our thoughts will help us to communicate with greater clarity thus avoiding ambiguity. Once our words are clearly defined and understood we may convey our thoughts with far fewer restrictions and greater force.

When communicating with us the concepts found in this passage of Scripture, Jesus chooses words that penetrate religious traditions, stripping every pretense and charade that holds men in spiritual and religious bondage. Jesus' choice of words is exact and accurate, bringing to bear life-changing concepts. "Shall not God avenge His own elect?" The word "avenge" is often shied away from in today's politically correct climate, but it is a good word pregnant with meaning. The word "avenge" means to vindicate a person's right or to avenge a thing. Simply put then, it means, "to make things right." Our God delights in making things right! After all, He is the Redeemer, the Rescuer, and the One Who makes all things right once again!

"Shall not God avenge His own elect?" The word "elect[12]" means to select, and by implication it means the favorite, the chosen, or the elect. Yes, God has favorites! While never respecting one person over the other because of social rank, race or gender – and while He is always fair, those who chose Him become the chosen, the favored of God, and the elect of God! To be sure, God's children are His elect and favored ones!

"*Put on therefore, as the elect of God, holy and beloved, bowels of mercies, kindness, humbleness of mind, meekness, longsuffering.*"
COLOSSIANS 3:12

God's elect will never suffer the disgrace of a fraudulent election poll or the humiliation of a recall.

"Shall not God avenge His own elect, which cry day and night unto Him?" The word "cry[13]" means far more than the shedding of a few tears! This word means to cry out for help in an impassioned and unrelenting manner. From the Amplified Bible we read,

So we take comfort and are encouraged and confidently and boldly say, 'The Lord is my Helper[14], I will not be seized with alarm - I will not fear or dread or be terrified! What can man do to me?

HEBREWS 13:6 AMPLIFIED

Almost every country has an emergency telephone number – typically three digits that when called are answered by trained professional who then dispatch emergency service to help. In the United States and Canada that phone number is 911. In Great Britain it is 999, and the Polish version is 997. The European standard emergency number is 112. The Australians dial 000 in an emergency and the Kiwis (New Zealanders) dial 111.

The Holy Spirit is also called the Helper in John's Gospel.

But the Helper, the Holy Spirit, whom the Father will send in My name, He will teach you all things, and bring to your remembrance all that I said to you.

JOHN 14:26 NASB

The Greek word for helper in this Scripture is Parakletos – which literally means "the one called along side to help."[15] This Divine Helper is always present and ready to assist and help us in our Christian walk. Now, this "Helper" in the book of Hebrews has a different nuance than that of John's writing. In Hebrews, He is the Boethos, which is the Greek word meaning "one who is poised and ready to rush to our aid when we cry for help."[16] Its meaning is not unlike the emergency worker, local police, fireman, or paramedic who is on call, standing by and ready to rush to our aid with sirens sounding and lights flashing – whenever we call. Respectfully then, we may say of the Holy Spirit, the Boethos Helper is our Divine 911 Emergency Number! Though ever present as our Helper and Comforter, whenever we will call upon the Name of Jesus, the Holy Spirit as the Boethos is poised and ready rush to our aid – with lights and sirens if necessary!

> *There is no one like the God of Jeshurun, Who rides the heavens to help you, and in His Excellency on the clouds. The eternal God is your refuge, and underneath are the everlasting arms... then Israel will dwell in safety."*
>
> DEUTERONOMY 33:26 – 28

"Faithful... faithful... faithful... fruit!"

Our next and final word definition is for the word speedily. "I tell you that He will avenge them speedily" The word "speedily[17]" does not mean what we traditionally think when we hear the word speedily. It does not necessarily mean quickly. Instead this specific Greek word holds a meaning that implies the necessity of our being in the right place at the right time in the right frame of mind! Or we might say for our purposes here, "being in the right place at the right time in the right faith frame of mind and heart." What a key then to our prayer success! The willingness to wait upon the Lord and further the willingness to prepare ourselves spiritually and emotionally, coupled with a yieldedness of heart enables the Lord to get us into the right place at the right time to be in position to receive His response or answer to our faith filled prayer!

"Faithful... faithful... faithful... fruit!"

Never, ever, give up!

How many believers have given up the moment before their bowl was filled and their answer poured out to the earth? How many times have we allowed circumstances to discourage us and we have fainted in well doing and thus we were robbed of our harvest?

Don't give up just now! Don't become discouraged in well doing! Keep filling your prayer bowls with faith. Keep diligently to your confession of faith. Remain constant. As you continue faithful, faithful, faithful, you will reap the fruit!

> *So don't get tired of doing what is good. Don't get discouraged and give up, for we will reap a harvest of blessing at the appropriate time.*
>
> GALATIANS 6:9 NLT

And the angel took the censer; and he filled it (your bowl of prayer) with the fire of the altar and threw it to the earth; and there followed peals of thunder and sounds and flashes of lightning and an earthquake.

REVELATION 8:5

Something is happening in the heavenlies. Answers to your prayers are at the door. The sound and smell of rain is in the air. It is the sound of Heaven's rain – an abundant rain of answers to years of intercessions! *"Faithful, faithful, faithful, fruit!"*

Will you be found faithful?

As we approach the final days of this earth's present condition and we face the coming of the Son of Man, we must ask ourselves if we will be found faithful.

Nevertheless when the Son of Man cometh, shall He find faith on the earth?

LUKE 18:8B

The various roots of the world's systems are coming to full and final fruit. Evil is making the final manifestations of its hateful rage against God and His highest creation — Man

Why do the nations rage and the people plot a vain thing? The kings of the earth set themselves, and the rulers take counsel together, against the LORD and against His Anointed, saying, "Let us break their bonds in pieces and cast away their cords from us." He who sits in the heavens shall laugh; the LORD shall hold them in derision. Then He shall speak to them in His wrath, and distress them in His deep displeasure. "Yet I have set My King on My holy hill of Zion." I will declare the decree: "The LORD has said to Me, 'You are My Son, today I have begotten You. Ask of Me, and I will give You The nations for Your inheritance, and the ends of the earth for Your possession. You shall break them with a rod of iron; You shall dash them to pieces like a potter's vessel.'" Now therefore, be wise, O kings; be instructed, you judges of the earth. Serve the LORD with fear, and rejoice with trembling. Kiss the Son, lest He be angry, and you perish in the way, When His wrath is kindled but a little. Blessed are all those who put their trust in Him.

PSALM 2

For those of us who are found in Christ, "the Amen, the Faithful, and True Witness," this hour will be our time to shine forth with great intensity! Our future as Christians is a very bright one. Born of the Father of Lights (James 1:17) so we too will shine forth in Jesus' life and light.

> *Arise, shine, for your light is come and the glory of the Lord is risen upon you!*
>
> ISAIAH 60:1

It is in this moment of History's final seconds that the fruit of all the ages is finally coming to full maturity and ripeness. Both evil and righteous harvests are growing in the earth concurrently.

> *He (Jesus) answered and said unto them, "He that sows the good seed is the Son of man; The field is the world; the good seed are the children of the Kingdom; but the tares are the children of the wicked one; the enemy that sowed them is the devil; the harvest is the end of the world; and the reapers are the angels... Then shall the righteous shine forth as the sun in the Kingdom of their Father. Who hath ears to hear, let him hear."*
>
> MATTHEW 13:37-43

"*Faithful, faithful, faithful, fruit!*"

"Go on, go on, go on!"

To experience having our prayers answered and thereby enabling us to enjoy both the personal blessing of the Lord as well as our then becoming a blessing to those around us, requires that we exercise diligent and patient endurance.

> *For ye have need of patience, that, after ye have done the will of God, ye might receive the promise.*
>
> HEBREWS 10:36

It is vitally important as well that we stand as the elect of God and take our rightful place as the children of God, praying confidently and looking expectantly for our prayer bowls to be filled and overflowing! Above all things then, get yourself positioned into that spiritual place where you are "in the right place at the right time in the right faith frame of mind and heart."

Richard Maton, was the long time teacher, dean of students and close associate of Samuel Howells at the Bible College of Wales located in Swansea, Wales, U.K. When encouraging his students to go deeper into the life of Christian perseverance and remain faithful to Jesus and the "Every Creature Vision," he wrote this simple poem to put an exclamation point on his lecture. It is appropriate for us as we press ever onward and upward into the things of God with a full expectation of our prayer bowls being filled and overflowing with dramatic answers!

Go on, go on, go on, go on;
Go on, go on, go on.
Go on, go on, go on, go on;
Go on, go on, go on.

Yes, dear Christian friend, "Go on!"
"Faithful... faithful... faithful... fruit!"

Prayers of Salvation
and the Holy Spirit Baptism

Yes, it is possible for you to know Jesus Christ in a personal manner! It is not enough to only hold a historical understanding or belief in Jesus Christ. Jesus said, "You must be born again" (John 3:7). You must possess a personal relationship with Christ, that is, a living faith and trust in Him. This relationship begins when you repent of your sin and rebellion and acknowledge your need of the Saviour.

That if you shall confess with your mouth the Lord Jesus, and shall believe in your heart that God hath raised Him from the dead, you shall be saved. For with the heart man believes unto righteousness; and with the mouth confession is made unto salvation.

ROMANS 10:9 – 10

"Father, today, I readily acknowledge my need of Jesus. I am a sinner and I need the Savior. I believe Jesus took my sin to the cross with Him. I believe He died in my place, carrying and bearing all of my sins and the punishments due me. I also believe that You raised Him from the dead that I might have new life – eternal life, in Him! Jesus is Lord. From this day forward, Jesus is my Lord! Alleluia!"

There's more!

If you prayed this prayer, the Bible says you are now born again. You are now a child of God – born of His Spirit. But God has even more for you. Jesus commanded His people to be baptized with the Holy Spirit.

Mark D. Spencer

"But you shall receive power, after that the Holy Spirit is come upon you: and you shall be witnesses unto Me both in Jerusalem, and in all Judaea, and in Samaria, and unto the uttermost part of the earth."

ACTS 1:8

Once you're born again, it's time to receive the empowering of the Holy Spirit. As Jesus baptizes you in the Holy Spirit you will begin to speak forth, not from your mind but from your spirit, a new language that will enable you to pray perfect prayers and worship the Lord, not only with your mind, but from your spirit. Are you ready? Then pray on...

"Lord Jesus, I believe Your Word and I now pray in obedience to Your Word for You to baptize me in the Holy Spirit. I expect to receive the baptism of the Holy Spirit with the evidence of speaking in other tongues as You promised I would. Thank You Lord for this empowering of the Spirit so that I may be a dynamic witness to my world of Your resurrection victory! I will expect miracles, signs and wonders to follow my testimony from this day forward, in Your name!

Alleluia!"

Now that you are born again and filled with the Spirit, tell someone what has happened to you. Commit to spending time daily in God's Word and with Him in prayer. Find a fellowship of Christians who dare to believe God's Word. Be ready to tell others about your Jesus and His great goodness and mercy. Spend time every day in fellowship with Him. Your world will never be the same!

End Notes

1   Basil Miller. *Charles Finney* (Minneapolis, MN Dimension Books) page 50
2   Found on a Fear God© t-shirt. See at www.feargod.com
3   The Webster's New Twentieth Century Dictionary Unabridged
4   Roget's International Thesaurus 240.2
5   Research News and Publications Office, Georgia Institute of Technology 75 Fifth Street, N.W., Suite 100, Atlanta, Georgia 30308 USA Article released on June 20, 2007 "65-Foot Waves: Scientists Report Study Results from "Stealth" Tsunami That Killed 600 in Java Last Summer" Found online at http://gtresearchnews. gatech.edu/newsrelease/java-tsunami.htm
6   See Chapter 9, "*The Season of Aaron's Rod*"
7   Mark D. Spencer *Surely God Will Do Me Good!* (Chapter 5, "*Of Tsunamis, God and Men...or from Whence Cometh Tragedy?*")
8   This prophetic word came to Mark in the Spring of 2003 while he was praying for Israel.
9   Hebrews 12:22-24 "But ye are come unto Mount Zion, and unto the city of the living God, the heavenly Jerusalem, and to an innumerable company of angels, To the general assembly and church of the firstborn, which are written in heaven, and to God the Judge of all, and to the spirits of just men made perfect, and to Jesus the mediator of the new covenant, and to the blood of sprinkling, that speaks better things than that of Abel."
10 When the "word of the Lord" comes, it must be judged primarily by the Word of God. We must also recognize that when such a word does come that it is so real and so personal to the one hearing it, that it can easily be mistaken for a personal word rather than a word that is to be given to the larger body of Christ. And so this too, must be discerned and ultimately recognized by the larger Body of Christ as such – a word for the entire body of Christ.
11 Eugene Peterson
12 *Strong's Exhaustive Concordance* #1588. eklektos, ek-lek-tos'; from G1586; select; by implication the favorite, chosen or elect.
13 *Strong's Exhaustive Concordance* #994. boao, to halloo, i.e. shout (for help or in a tumultuous way):-cry.
14 The Greek word for Helper used in this instance is different than the use in John 14:16 NASB "And I will ask the Father, and He will give you another Helper, that He may be with you forever." We are more familiar with the term Parakletos,

par-ak'-lay-tos; which means an intercessor, consoler:--advocate, comforter. One meaning for the word Paraklete is One who comes along side to help. However, in this passage in Hebrews we see the Helper as the Boethos – bah-ay-thoss – That is, the Beothos is the One who comes running when we cry for help. It pictures for us the Lord as poised and ready to rush to our aid and relief when we cry for His help!

[15] *Strong's Exhaustive Concordance* #3875

[16] *Strong's Exhaustive Concordance* #998. Also from the Word Wealth at Hebrews 13:6 found in the *Spirit-filled Life Bible*, Thomas Nelson Publishers,.

[17] *Strong's Exhaustive Concordance* #1722. en, en; denoting (fixed) position (in place, time or state)...

About the Author

Mark D. Spencer B.A., M.B.S., Th.D.

Mark is an internationally recognized pastor and teacher who ministers regularly in the US and abroad, challenging believers to a mature and uncompromising walk with God and a life centered in the Word of God and prayer. Founder of Inner Court Ministries and co-founder of Brotherhood Beyond Boundaries (a ministry of mutual encouragement with ministry leaders throughout Eastern Europe), Mark has served the Body of Christ in full-time ministry for more than 33 years. Mark holds degrees in Biblical Studies and Music Education. And while an accomplished musician, his great joy and focus are found in the high calling of "souls from every nation." Mark lives in Colorado with his wife Patty where they pastor Christ Church International as well as lead a dedicated group of prophetic intercessors. They have three grown sons, Joshua, Matthew and Jesse.

Mark's insightful through-the-Bible devotional *Before the Throne – the Devotional* is currently available on-line at www.feargod.com and www. innercourt.com. Other ministry helps may be found at www.innercourt. com as well as www.wheatlandstudios.com. Mark may be contacted at mark@innercourt.com or by mail at Mark Spencer, P.O. Box 2125, Longmont, Colorado, 80502-2125, USA.